SPORT CLIMBING
From Top Rope to Redpoint,
Techniques for Climbing Success

MOUNTAINEERS
OUTDOOR EXPERT
series

SPORT CLIMBING
From Top Rope to Redpoint, Techniques for Climbing Success

Andrew Bisharat

THE MOUNTAINEERS BOOKS

THE MOUNTAINEERS BOOKS
is the nonprofit publishing arm of The Mountaineers Club,
an organization founded in 1906 and dedicated to the exploration,
preservation, and enjoyment of outdoor and wilderness areas.

1001 SW Klickitat Way, Suite 201, Seattle, WA 98134

First edition, 2009

Distributed in the United Kingdom by Cordee, www.cordee.co.uk
Manufactured in the United States of America

Copy Editor: Colin Chisholm
Book Design: The Mountaineers Books
Layout: Marge Mueller/Gray Mouse Graphics
Illustrator: Jeremy Collins
All photographs by author unless credited otherwise.
Cover photograph: *Sam Elias makes the clip on* Rumor Has It *(5.11b), Rifle, Colorado.* © Chris Hunter/www
.HunterImagery.com
Back cover photograph: Berta Martin finds repose and relaxation amid a steep 5.13d in Spain. Photo © Keith
Ladzinski/www.ladzinski.com
Frontispiece: *Lauren Lee cranks* Blue Bard *(5.13a), La Glacier, France.* © Keith Ladzinski
Additional photographs provided by Boone Speed/www.boonespeed.com, David Clifford/www.davidclifford
photography.com, Andy Mann/www.andymann.com, and Marni Mattner/www.mattnerphotography.com

Library of Congress Cataloging-in-Publication Data
Bisharat, Andrew, 1981-
  Sport climbing : from top rope to redpoint, techniques for climbing success / by Andrew Bisharat ; foreword
  by Chris Sharma. -- 1st ed.
      p. cm.
  Includes bibliographical references and index.
  ISBN 978-1-59485-270-1 (alk. paper)
  1. Rock climbing. 2. Free climbing. I. Title.
  GV200.2.B56 2009
  796.522'4--dc22
                                    2009019827

Contents

Acknowledgments

I'd like to thank, first and foremost, my many (and far more talented) climbing partners, who have not only taught me everything I know, but who have made sport climbing such a powerful life passion. There are too many to list, but special acknowledgments must be paid to Jen Vennon, Sam Elias, Dan Mirsky, Dan Robertson, Wendy Williams, and Joe Kinder. Thanks to my writing mentors, co-workers, and editors at *Rock and Ice*: Duane Raleigh, Jeff Jackson, and Alison Osius—without their support and guidance this would not have happened. Thanks to my editors at The Mountaineers Books: Kate Rogers, Mary Metz, and Colin Chisholm, and their excellent work. Special thanks to Keith Ladzinski, David Clifford, Andy Mann, Marni Mattner, and Boone Speed—the photographers whose excellent work appears in this book and continues to provide inspiration to and instill dreams in the climbing community. Much thanks and great respect to Chris Sharma, first for writing this book's foreword, but also for raising standards and bringing the rest of us up with him. Thanks to the talented climbers, who not only inspire me, but who contributed to the techniques and ideas formulated in this book, especially Dave Graham, Ethan Pringle, Daniel Woods, Dani Andrada, Lee Sheftel, Matt Samet, Bill Ramsey, Tommy Caldwell, Lynn Hill, Jon Cardwell, Alex Honnold, and Emily Harrington. Thanks to Mike Call for his support. Finally, I want to thank all of the sport's route developers for their gift to the community: the sport climbs that have given the rest of us such enjoyment, passion, and purpose. Their blood, sweat, and tears (not to mention time and money) is much appreciated.

Foreword

THE FULL CIRCLE

When I started climbing in 1994, bouldering was just blowing up and no one had even heard of deep-water soloing, but the sport-climbing revolution was in full effect. All of the work done by the early sport-climbing pioneers—discovering new cliffs, developing trails, and bolting hundreds of routes—appeared to be paying off. Those climbers, despite their atrocious fashion sense, were free climbing harder than anyone had ever imagined.

Three years before, in 1991, Wolfgang Güllich, of Germany, had set the bar high with the world's first 5.14d, *Action Directe*, on his home turf. Then, in 1992, the French climber J.B. Tribout established the first 5.14c on U.S. soil: *Just Do It*, at Smith Rock, Oregon. Each year more routes emerged on longer sweeping faces with super-complex, athletic moves that just *flowed* into each other. Those routes and the climbers who freed them inspired and motivated me most in those initial years. (I never understood the Lycra tights, however.)

I continued to cut my teeth sport climbing, but increasingly found myself being pulled toward the boulders. First and foremost, I've always been intrigued by

Chris Sharma making short work of the insta-classic 50 Words for Pump *(5.14c), Red River Gorge, Kentucky* (Photo © Keith Ladzinski)

cool, gymnastic movement on rock—this is what bouldering is all about. I'd go out each day and try to pull as hard as I could on the smallest holds possible, if only to see just how hard a single three-move sequence could be. Bouldering is amazing: no ropes or gear—it's just you and the rock. It is simultaneously the simplest and the most complex type of climbing there is.

After bouldering almost exclusively for years, in 2004 I took a trip to the Spanish island Mallorca to try my hand at the relatively new sport called "deep-water soloing," which is climbing up sea cliffs with nothing but the turbulent ocean waves to keep you safe if you fall. The locals in Mallorca, however, call it *psicobloc,* as in "psycho bouldering," an apt name since it feels more like an extension of bouldering than anything else.

Discovering *psicobloc* really brought me a whole new level of motivation. To have the sea as a crash pad gives you the freedom to explore any cliff (up to about 60 feet) as you wish. Unlike a sport climb, which has bolts and an anchor at its end, there is no delineated path in *psicobloc.* In one fraction of a second you go from climbing on this solid thing, this earth, to floating in its polar opposite. All of the elements are there: the stone, the air when you're falling, the water, and the fire inside.

While *psicobloc* is really similar to bouldering, cliffs of these heights are really more like sport climbs. During my stint in Mallorca, climbing over the Mediterranean Sea, I found myself reconnecting to the flow of continuous movement and the fight of being pumped out of your mind—exalting sensations experienced only on hard sport routes. Deep-water soloing ignited something within, and I unexpectedly felt myself being pulled back to sport climbing. In this sense, I've come full circle, back to my "routes."

As of 2009 I've been sport climbing exclusively, yet things have changed over the years. Everything I've learned from bouldering and relearned from deep-water soloing has made me feel as if I am seeing sport climbing with new eyes.

What does it look like? Routes that aren't just a ladder of holds, but demand that you really dig deep to unlock bouldery sequences; the fluidity of moving up a big, bad cliff; and the strategy needed to connect the moves before the ticking time bomb of your forearms explodes. Finally, it means giving back to the community through the creative process of bolting and climbing new routes. It's something I find extremely satisfying on all levels.

As I get older, there's one thing I appreciate about sport climbing more than anything: its friendliness on the body. While bouldering is all about holding on as hard as you can to the smallest, most painful holds, sport climbing allows you to breathe and relax. You connect to the rock with as little grip—both mental and physical—as possible in order to conserve your energy. It's a type of climbing for all ages and all levels, and it's never too late to start. I know many people in their mid-fifties who climb 5.14, and some of them didn't start climbing until they were in their late thirties.

The true essence of sport climbing means giving 100 percent, regardless of how hard you climb. Some of the most inspiring climbers I know project 5.11 routes, but their motivation is pure and they love what they're doing. In the end, it's all about having a good time with your friends, being in a beautiful place, and doing a little climbing.

Sport Climbing: From Top Rope to Redpoint, Techniques For Climbing Success not only offers the modern techniques you need to get started, but provides tips to improve throughout your climbing career. Take the time to enjoy the process and to be safe, and hopefully your climbing will come full circle, too.

—Chris Sharma

Chris Sharma is one of the world's best sport climbers. He did the first ascents of such iconic routes as Realization *(5.15a) and* Jumbo Love *(5.15b). Orginally from Santa Cruz, California, Sharma now lives wherever his quest for fine rock takes him.*

INTRODUCTION

SPORT CLIMBING:
THE NEXT ERA OF ASCENT

Sylvain Millet was in silhouette against the dying light at Céüse. The famously blue, pocketed wall that distinguishes this French crag glowed coolly in the evening. Millet racked four—*just four*—draws on his harness in preparation to climb the 120-foot route. On this night, in the summer of 2006, the quiet Frenchman tied in, then spit on his hand and mashed his fleshy palm into the sole of his climbing shoe, cleaning the rubber until it squeaked dry. He took a deep breath and began.

The route was a 5.13a called *All Is Not So Easy*, but for Millet, who had climbed the illustrious *Realization*—one of the world's hardest routes with a rating of 5.15a—it was relatively easy. Millet was only interested in reaching his project, a 50-foot extension to *All Is Not So Easy* that might be as difficult as 5.13d. Millet had *All Is Not So Easy* so wired that he climbed 30 feet up the wall before taking a quickdraw from his harness and clipping into a bolt. For Millet, stopping to clip would have interrupted his flow and movement. Not only that, but clipping sapped critical strength, and if Millet hoped to redpoint his project, he could not be pumped.

After successfully climbing the 5.13a, Millet paused to shake the lactic acid out of his forearms and to prepare for the remaining difficulties. As Millet moved up into the crux he reminded himself to stay composed, to set his feet accurately, and to hang off the shallow dishes and hard edges with straight arms and a minimal

Roman Gershkovich taking care of a classic 5.13a at one of the world's best sport-climbing crags, Céüse, France (Photo © Keith Ladzinski)

grip. He moved slowly but constantly—in balance and with total efficiency. Twenty feet below the anchor and 20 feet *above* his last protection, Millet cranked hard off of his right arm and released a guttural blast, "Psaaaaht!" The crowd of climbers beneath cringed anxiously. Would he battle through and succeed, or would he take the fall?

That day Millet pitched, gently arcing through the air for 50 feet before his thin rope softly caught his fall. He lowered to the ground as the last rays of light washed up the wall. Millet smiled. Success would come another day. The route wasn't going anywhere.

WHAT IS SPORT CLIMBING?

Sport climbing is a style of rock climbing during which the climber relies on the safety of preexisting or "fixed" protection, usually bolts that have been drilled into the wall. With fixed protection, sport climbing is considered the safest form of rock climbing. A solid bolt placed in good rock is safe and reliable, allowing sport climbers to focus on pushing their free-climbing skills without worrying too much about the consequences of a fall. The emphasis in sport climbing is less on managing danger and risk, and more on pushing physical boundaries. The primary goal is to free climb an entire pitch, leading it from start to end without falling or resting on gear.

FUNDAMENTAL TERMS

Route. A route is a definitive path up a cliff. Sport routes (or climbs) have a certain number of bolts in them, and usually a two-bolt anchor at the end. The goal is to reach the anchor without falling. Routes are given names (which appear in this book in italics) as well as a free-climbing grade such as "5.10a."

Crag. A crag is a cliff with a collection of routes of various grades and quality. Typically, climbers use guidebooks to find crags and the particular routes there.

Free climbing. A general term that simply means you are relying on your hands and feet—not gear—to actually move up a wall. Gear is used, but only to keep you safe if you fall. Free climbing is the opposite of *aid climbing*, which involves a climber placing gear and hanging from it in order to progress upward. Many climbers consider free climbing to be the purest form of climbing. Gymnastic moves allow free climbers to move up a sheer face, using only the natural hand- and footholds presented by the rock.

Free climbing is not exclusive to one particular discipline of rock climbing—it can be done on tiny boulders with no gear, or on big walls with a rope and lots of gear. This is an important distinction because free climbing is often confused with "free soloing," which means free climbing a tall route *without* the safety of a rope or gear.

While certainly physically challenging, free climbing engages the mind equally. A climber must figure out how to "read" a route—what sequence to grab the holds, how and when to grab them, how to best place the feet, and so on. There's also the thrill of leading above your gear and risking a fall—and then learning how to balance this fear with an ability to remain calm and climb well, like Sylvain Millet, who eventually "sent" (aka redpointed) the project described above. Finally, there's the mental barrier of believing you can actually climb something you once found impossible. Sometimes this feels like the greatest challenge of all.

Leading. Climbing "on lead" or "leading a climb" is the act of ascending a route from the ground to the top. A leader clips the rope to the preplaced bolts using "quickdraws," which are two carabiners attached via a nylon sling (one carabiner clips to the bolt, while the other clips to the rope). After clipping the quickdraw to the bolt, then the rope to the quickdraw, the leader must climb above his "protection" to reach the next bolt. Climbing above one's last protection means risking a lead fall, which is a fall roughly twice the distance above a bolt. If a leader is three feet above a bolt and he falls, he will fall a total of six feet before the belayer can catch him. If he is 5 feet above a bolt, he faces a 10-foot fall. Falls in climbing are arrested by your partner, the "belayer," who uses a belay device to hold the rope and catch the lead climber.

Top rope. The opposite of leading, a top rope involves running the rope through the anchor at the top of the route and down to a climber. Thus, the climber always has the rope above him to catch a fall. As the climber climbs up, the belayer takes in the rope through the belay device. Top-roping

is a good way to safely become comfortable climbing up a vertical wall. That said, a top-rope ascent doesn't actually "count" as an ascent. Beginners who are uncomfortable leading most often top-rope to enjoy and to experience free climbing. Also, top-roping is a popular way to "run laps" on routes, and get in a quick workout.

Beta. This is information about a route: how to do the moves, where crucial hand- or footholds are, route length or location, or anything that could be deemed useful to a free climber. The term was coined in the mid-1980s by the great climber Jack Mileski, who is fondly remembered by his climbing partners for being so excited about climbing that he simply couldn't help sharing his way of doing moves with other climbers who were up on a route. "Beta" is thought to be short for Betamax, the video format that was eventually replaced by VHS, and its correlation to climbing was possibly a reference to being able to rewind video—or "replay" moves. We'll never really know since Mileski was tragically murdered in 1997 by his ex-girlfriend. However, his quirky term—and his passion for helping people climb—lives on.

Sending, or an "ascent." Sport climbing's point is to "send" a route—that is, to make a successful "free ascent" of it—which means leading a climb without resting on gear. Successful free ascents can be categorized as an onsight, flash, or redpoint.

- **Onsight.** This means free climbing a route on the first try without any prior knowledge of it. An onsight is the purest style of ascent you can make, and it is the ultimate goal of any route you choose. Most climbers will only onsight routes that are easy for them, though even on easy climbs, an onsight is not guaranteed. You only get one shot to onsight a climb, which is what makes it so special.

- **Flash.** Like an onsight, a flash is also a successful *first-try ascent* of a route; however, a flash differs in that the climber has beta, particularly knowing where the crux is, how to grab certain key holds, or having someone tell you what to do from the ground. Flashing is the second-best style of ascent you can make, and sometimes climbers try to flash routes—gathering as much beta beforehand as possible—that they think would be too hard for them to onsight.
- **Redpoint.** This means successfully ascending a route that you have tried and failed on before. Redpointing is the most common style used by sport climbers who "work" on one particular climb that is hard for them until they have figured out all the moves and have the strength and fitness to link them together. Sport climbing's backbone is the redpoint style of ascent.

Project. First and foremost a "project" means a route that has been tried but not successfully redpointed by anyone. However, in today's vernacular, climbers use the word "project" when talking about a route that *they themselves* are trying to redpoint—even if others have done it before them. To wit: "How's your project going?" "Not bad. I've *only* fallen thirty times at the same move. Hopefully I'll do it next try!"

Hangdogging. This is the name given to working a project by hanging on the bolts in order to figure out the free-climbing moves. A climber hangdogs a project with the intention of one day redpointing it.

Trad climbing. Trad, or traditional climbing, differs from sport climbing by the type of protection used. Trad climbers place their own protection—typically cams and nuts—in natural rock features. The protection is then removed when the second climber ascends the pitch. As in sport climbing, trad climbers *free climb*; however, they typically choose routes that are easier to free climb to compensate for the added difficulties and increased risk of placing one's own protection. The terms onsight, flash, and redpoint are also used in trad climbing.

Bouldering. When free climbing on boulders, no gear or ropes are used, except for crash pads. In bouldering, the point is not to simply reach the top; it's *how* you get there. Often boulderers seek the most difficult path, or "problem," they can find on a particular boulder in order to improve their free climbing. Whereas sport climbing tests a climber's endurance, bouldering is often a test of power. The hardest single free-climbing moves in the world are found on today's cutting-edge boulder problems.

GRADES

Grades are the funny-looking number/letter combinations that often follow a route's name in guidebooks and text. They are meant to provide a general idea of a route's free-climbing difficulty. Explaining grades is further complicated by the fact that there are at least a dozen different grading systems, not just among the many disciplines of climbing (such as bouldering, rock, bigwall, ice) but among different countries and regions.

In North American free climbing the grading scale used is the Yosemite Decimal System (YDS), which looks like this: "5.9" or "5.11c."

The system derives out of a larger system that grades the technical difficulty of hiking trails. A Class 1 trail is a flat walk, while a Class 3 is steep and may involve using your hands to scramble over or around boulders. Class 4 is like Class 3, only it's more exposed, meaning there's a danger of falling off a cliff. Class 5 means that the "trail" becomes so steep and technical that you need ropes and gear to safely go up it. Class 5 is the start of technical free climbing, which is why YDS grades begin with a "5," followed by a decimal, followed by another number or number/letter combo.

The YDS is an open-ended system, meaning there's no cap to how difficult a rock climb can be. The scale begins at 5.1, and goes 5.2, 5.3 . . . all the way up to 5.9. Things get complicated at 5.10, at which point climbs are further broken down by the letters "a," "b," "c," and "d." To wit: 5.10a, 5.10b, 5.10c, 5.10d, 5.11a, and so on.

For sport climbing, beginner-level routes are in the 5.1 to 5.9 range. 5.10a to 5.11d routes are considered "moderate," and are a good range for intermediate-level climbers.

5.12a is where advanced climbing begins. For most people of average fitness with honed climbing technique, 5.12 and even 5.13a are reasonable goals. Climbing 5.13 + and 5.14 require not only above-average fitness, but superb climbing technique. As of 2009 the hardest routes in the world are rated 5.15b.

Sometimes, instead of letters, you will see a plus or minus sign. This is simply a way to remain vague when a grade isn't certain. For example 5.13 + means, "Hard 5.13, let's just leave it at that." Likewise, 5.9- means "an easier 5.9."

With ratings of certain trad climbs, you will sometimes see the YDS grade paired with an "R" or "X." These two letters provide information about how dangerous a route is to lead. "R" means there are significant "runouts" between reliable protection points. In other words, a leader has to climb farther above his last protection piece before reaching the next one. An R-rated route exposes a leader to a long fall that could be injurious. "X" is like "R," except that the runouts are much longer. There are dire consequences to falling on an X-rated route.

Grades are far from an exact science, and they are not supposed to be taken too seriously or literally. Grades are merely meant to give you a rough estimate of what kind of challenges you can expect. Climbs are graded by the climber who makes the first ascent, and thus may be far from objective. One man's 5.10a may be another man's 5.9. Similarly, you may surprise yourself and find that, even though you've only ever climbed a 5.9, there are some 5.10c's that are well within your abilities.

The jump in difficulty from 5.8 to 5.9 is meant to be equivalent to the jump in difficulty from 5.10a to 5.10b, or 5.11d to 5.12a. However, you'll find it's far easier to make quicker progress through the lower grades than the higher ones—this is merely a function of the learning curve. When starting out, gaining the technical skills, poise, and balance needed to rock climb a moderate route comes faster than gaining the new level of fitness (endurance and power) needed to take your redpoint level to the next grade.

Onsight vs. redpoint grades. These vague terms help explain the variation of grading that occurs for different climbs at different areas. The person who "establishes a route" (drills its bolts and redpoints it first) also gets to grade the climb. Subsequent repeats may reveal that the original grade is too high or too low. Climbers are like upward-flowing water: always finding the easiest path to the top. Grades can be influenced by anything, from ego, to a guidebook author wanting grades that make people feel good, to ignorance, to personal strengths and weaknesses. Typically routes are rated relative to the other routes in that area. If there are a bunch of 5.11d routes and someone establishes a route that feels noticeably harder, he might rate it 5.12a— even though, if it were in another area, it might be 5.12b or even 5.11c!

An "onsight grade" is the degree of difficulty a typical climber will experience during the onsight, whereas a "redpoint grade" means that the route has been graded to reflect the degree of difficulty a climber will experience with perfect beta during the redpoint.

At most sport-climbing areas, the "moderate grades," or anything under 5.11, are graded for the onsight. Most trad routes use onsight grades as well.

As climbs get harder, or at areas with routes that are difficult to onsight, redpoint grades are more commonly employed. An area boasting redpoint grades often feels harder at first.

THE ELITE DECEIT

Sport climbing can be challenging to a person's self esteem. It's *hard*, and people don't like failing. Many climbers would rather spend a day onsighting easier routes than projecting a route beyond their current ability. Discouragement may be exacerbated when a climber sees other climbers easily doing routes that he struggles with. However, this attitude is often the result of common misperceptions about how hard routes are achieved.

It's easy to feel like there's an enormous gap between what you do and what the pros do when climbing magazines and videos rarely show the featured talents failing.

During my tenure as a senior editor at *Rock and Ice*, I've been fortunate enough to actually climb with and watch the world's best in action. It's not only true that good sport climbers fail, but that they fail *a lot*. I've seen Tommy Caldwell take half an hour to manage an easy boulder problem.

I belayed Chris Sharma when he asked me to "Take!" on a 5.13a that he had done many times years before. I've seen Dave Graham quiver with fear on a 5.10, and I've witnessed countless 5.14 climbers struggle on easy 5.11 routes. Everyone has bad days, but it's the great days in sport climbing that are so rare and special. That's because free climbing is just plain hard.

Undoubtedly, genetics and natural talent help a person become good, but success in sport climbing is equally about having the right attitude and knowing the right tactics and techniques.

So, what is it that makes Chris Sharma, Tommy Caldwell, Dave Graham, and all the other 5.14 crushers so good? The biggest difference that separates "us" from "them" is their *willingness to fail,* and their desire to learn from mistakes, improve weaknesses, stay positive, and, above all, be persistent. If you can accept that you will be doing more falling and failing, and actually enjoy this process, then every day you get out will be great. Accept that sport climbing is a tremendous, lifelong challenge—embrace it—and you will continue to improve indefinitely. One day you'll be clipping the chains after onsighting another 5.12, shaking your head and grinning wildly with disbelief at how far you've come.

A NEW LOOK

Sport climbing is the art of free climbing at its pinnacle. No other free-climbing discipline demands more of your strength, stamina, power, and mental acuity than successfully redpointing a sport climb that is truly difficult for you.

Of course, at its heart, *sport climbing is just plain fun*. Anything more is vanity. Yet it's hard to deny that sport climbing is at once uplifting and demanding, moral and enlightening, and an infinite challenge.

The rise of standards over just the last decade, along with the emergence of thousands of new routes and hundreds of user-friendly crags, has changed the face of sport climbing so drastically that an anthology of gear, tactics, belay skills, and ropework techniques have been developed and modified to tackle these modern challenges.

This book intends to define the new face of this exceptional discipline, and to address both the basics for getting started as well as the cutting-edge strategies that climbers use to redpoint routes at their physical and mental limits. These techniques will help any climber on any route, regardless of whether it's 5.8 or 5.15.

There are no boundaries in sport climbing, personal or otherwise. Sport climbing could mean a carefree day spent hammering out a bunch of routes with close friends. Its logistical ease and accessibility make even three hours at a well-developed crag a great workout and a satisfying afternoon—much appreciated by those with full-time jobs and busy lives. Says Jim Gilchrist, a longtime climber and high-school principal, "If it weren't for sport climbing, I don't know if I'd be climbing anymore!" Sport climbing allows him to stay in shape for climbing road trips.

Sport climbing can also involve heading up a route so difficult you can barely do the moves on your first attempt. Redpointing the route may require months of dedicating every free weekend to "working your project" and gaining the fitness to do it. This can be a frustrating ordeal, but when you succeed, you'll feel unbelievably content...for about a week. You will celebrate, but only a bit. The next climb always beckons, and the process begins again.

No matter how seriously you take it, or what grade you climb, there is one underlying truth that you will hear repeated throughout this book: sport climbing is the very best way to improve your abilities as a rock climber. Training in the gym, losing weight, slapping a campus board—these things can be good (in moderation), but they pale in comparison to the real-world powers that dedicated sport climbing brings.

These days, every great all-around climber has a strong background in sport climbing. It is one of the main reasons Tommy Caldwell has freed more routes on El Cap than anyone else and Alex Honnold has the fitness and skill to free solo big walls such as the *Regular Route* (5.12a) on Half Dome and the *Moonlight Buttress* (5.12d) in Zion.

Sport climbing is immensely rewarding in and of itself. Yes, it's culturally taboo to "chase grades," but seeing yourself progress from 5.8 to 5.10 to 5.12 to 5.14 (why not?) is certainly gratifying. It takes a lot of work to go from 5.10a to 5.11a, and even more work to go from 5.12d to 5.13a, but it's usually true that the more work you put into something, the more rewarding the process becomes.

Finally, always remember this: At some point, *everyone struggles to succeed.* Herein lies the social cement that binds climbers of all levels and makes us one. Find true happiness in your friends' successes, and they will revel in yours. If you can balance your passion to improve with a moderating sense of humility and goodwill, you will have succeeded beyond any redpoint.

A NOTE ABOUT SAFETY

Safety is an important concern in all outdoor activities. No book can alert you to every hazard or anticipate the limitations of every reader. The descriptions of techniques and procedures in this book are intended to provide general information. This is not a complete text on climbing or training technique. Nothing substitutes for formal instruction, routine practice, and plenty of experience. When you follow any of the procedures described here, you assume responsibility for your own safety. Use this book as a general guide to further information. Under normal conditions, excursions into the backcountry require attention to traffic, road and trail conditions, weather, terrain, the capabilities of your party, and other factors. Keeping informed on current conditions and exercising common sense are the keys to a safe, enjoyable outing.

The Mountaineers Books

CHAPTER 1

Sam Elias hanging tough on Graphique (5.13b), located in the place where it all started, the Verdon, France (Photo © Keith Ladzinski)

Ethics, Style, and the Emergence of Sport Climbing

To understand sport climbing, it helps to know the history: its departure from traditional climbing, the ethical debates it yielded, and the emergence of the modern version of the sport. Knowing the history will give you a conceptual foundation of ethics and style, not to mention a deeper appreciation of how lucky we are to have so many well-equipped sport crags.

The two most commonly misused words in climbing's quirky language have to be *style* and *ethics*. Style refers to how a climber chooses to tackle a vertical challenge. Inherently it's neither good nor bad, but just a description of what one does so long as the actions do not affect others. Style could mean top-roping a route before leading it, or preclipping the first two bolts with a stick clip—both styles are fine if that's how someone wishes to climb. Styles are subjective, and different climbers value various styles. That said, top-roping a route first (for example) is an inferior style to, say, an onsight ascent.

Ethics contain inherent judgments and can be placed on a spectrum of "good" and "bad." Ethics (or lack thereof) determine actions that exist on a broad spectrum—from placing tickmarks to chipping holds to lying about the style of ascent used.

Our climbing culture has adopted imprecise language that defines *trad climbing* as placing gear and *sport climbing* as clipping bolts. Though that's more or less true, traditional climbing started out as a *style* of climbing that mandated starting on the ground with no knowledge of the route, and placing protection on lead. The opposite style—top-roping or inspecting gear from the top down—was called "sport

THE BEAST CAME FROM TRAD

climbing." Historically, trad-climbing ethics aimed to leave the rock in the most natural state possible. Fixing gear, placing bolts, and even using chalk were all ethical transgressions in trad climbing because they affected the experience of fellow climbers. Before gear innovations such as cams, however, pitons were used in traditional climbing even though they scarred the rock.

Today trad climbing refers more to the type of gear used rather than the style of ascent. It means placing and removing natural protection on lead, with minimal impact to the rock. Above all, the most important distinction between trad and sport climbing is how the protection is placed in the rock, and whether the protection is temporary or fixed.

THE BEAST CAME FROM TRAD

In the 1970s Yosemite Valley was the epicenter of free climbing, and within this granite crucible a set of "rules" was created to accompany the rapidly developing game called rock climbing. Back then it was all about *ground-up first ascents*. Climbers started on the ground, sought out the tallest routes, and went up, trying to free climb as often as possible. While some version of these "rules" had been in place since the birth of mountaineering, they were refined in Yosemite to pertain to the area's geology: perfect granite, splitter cracks, and big walls. Due to Yosemite's prominence, the

greater climbing community adopted these ethics, even in places that, unlike Yosemite, didn't have bomber rock conducive to placing natural protection.

Not every rock face took natural or "clean" protection, and sometimes placing bolts was the only way to make a route safe. As long as the bolts were placed ground-up (i.e., on lead), onsight, and from stances, drilling bolts was usually tolerated. This type of bolt placement also fell within the realm of "traditional" climbing even though the route incorporated fixed gear.

In 1981 John Bachar employed this style on the *Bachar-Yerian* (5.11c R) in Tuolumne Meadows. While protected by fixed bolts, the *Bachar-Yerian* is definitely not a sport climb because it's dangerously runout and Bachar drilled the bolts on lead. Still, Bachar's ascent was controversial because in three instances on sections of the route too thin and steep to place the bolts from stances, Bachar hung from hooks he delicately placed over slippery knobs. After installing those bolts, he lowered down and started over, releading the runout climbing until he reached the top of Medlicott Dome.

Imagine for a second the boldness and sheer *adventure* of it. Picture climbing up the blank face, not knowing if there are going to be holds in 10 or 50 feet, but sure as the day is long you know there's no fixed protection up there. Bachar risked severe injury because he believed in this style: climbing ground-up and minimizing fixed gear.

Establishing routes in this style didn't

make sense everywhere and for everyone, especially in one birthplace of sport climbing: Les Gorges du Verdon, France. The Verdon has been called the Grand Canyon of limestone, and you approach this magnificent 2000-foot blue chasm from a road that runs along its rim. In the early 1960s climbers had been developing routes here in traditional Yosemite style: walking down to the canyon floor, seeking the easiest-looking features such as vertical cracks that would most obviously take removable protection (e.g. nuts, pitons, and hexes), and going up.

Around the late 1970s, however, French climbers such as Stephane Troussier and Christian Guyomar abandoned these stylistic constraints in order to test themselves on the Verdon's alluring crackless faces. Exploring from the top-down just made more sense in an area where you start at the top of the cliff anyway. It was an obvious solution to wanting to have more routes to climb—as many as possible—and not wanting to drill bolts from hooks, ground-up, and without pre-inspection. Bolting routes ground-up, when you aren't really sure where (or if) the line goes, can result in poor bolt placements. Despite being bolted on rappel, none of the early Verdon experiments are grid-bolted *giveaways*. Celebrated routes such as *Pichenibule* (5.12c), *Les Rideaux de Gwendal* (5.12b), and *L'age de Raison* (5.12c) are stiff for their grades and boast 30-foot runouts.

The United States lagged behind the Europeans in the progression of top-down sport climbing, but one innovator moved the country in that direction by introducing "hangdogging." An original tenet of trad style dictated that if a leader fell, he should start over from the ground and relead the route before continuing past the point of failure. Hangdogging—resting on gear in order to work out the moves—was a faux pas and downright cheating.

In 1977 Ray Jardine, who invented cams (also originally considered cheating because, compared to hexes, they were too easy to place), was one of the first to employ hangdogging techniques on the first ascent of *Phoenix,* Yosemite's first 5.13a. Jardine used his mechanical widgets, cheerfully named "Friends," to protect the overhanging splitter adjacent to Cascade Falls. *Phoenix* is sustained and pumpy, and while Jardine technically free-climbed each and every move of the crack, he hung from Friends three times during his "free ascent" (he originally said his style warranted a grade of only 5.12d).

Jardine was an infamous, controversial figure, and for many he will be remembered poorly for chipping holds into a pitch on the *Nose* of El Cap. Yet the "Jardine Traverse," however unethical, is also the path all climbers now use to free climb this mega-classic. While the merits of his actions are debatable, no one will disagree that Jardine significantly influenced the progression of free climbing. His cams revolutionized trad, and his hangdogging technique—which he dubbed "working the route"—was a stylistic innovation that paved a path for free climbers to approach difficult terrain.

In 1979 Tony Yaniro established the traditionally protected *Grand Illusion* (5.13c), then the hardest free climb in the world. Located at Sugar Loaf, outside of South Lake Tahoe, California, *Grand Illusion* is a stunning line. Yaniro hangdogged the route to work the moves, and later that year he appeared on a magazine cover climbing *Grand Illusion*. For the climbing community it was mind-blowing. Many had never seen what hard 5.13 climbing looked like, and the captivating image was further justification that hangdogging might not be such a bad idea if it meant that something so outrageous could be climbed.

While the Verdon and especially the legendary French crag Buoux are credited with introducing the world to top-down bolt-protected rock climbing, American sport climbing didn't kick off until 1983 when Alan Watts established *Watts Tots* (5.12b) at Smith Rock, Oregon. Like every other climber back then, Watts played by Yosemite's rules of style and ethics, but he departed from tradition by drilling *Watts Tots* on rappel. It was his solution to the friable nature of Smith's blank faces. (Of course, Smith was a traditional area—only after most of the area's cracks had been climbed did Smith legends like Watts, Chris Jones, Chris Grover, Bill Ramsey, and Alan Lester look for new challenges on the blanker faces.)

In *A Climber's Guide to Smith Rock*, Watts wrote, "My decision to break with tradition wasn't a visionary act by any stretch of the imagination. Instead, it seemed like a sneaky way of putting up more routes. I never cared for the misery of starting up first ascents on Smith tuff from the ground, snapping holds and pulling off blocks along the way. Eliminating the dangers beforehand only seemed logical."

What Watts didn't predict was how greatly his "sneaky" tactics would divide and conquer American rock climbing over the next ten years.

SPORT CLIMBING IS NEITHER!?

"Sport climbing," as it was subsequently dubbed, emerged as a stylistic antithesis to trad climbing (before then, trad climbing was just called "climbing"). Sport climbing is a style of establishing a route from the top down, placing bolts (or gear) first on rappel, pre-inspecting holds, or using hangdogging techniques to work toward an eventual free ascent, or "redpoint."

Ethically, to those who wanted to establish climbs ground-up, sport style was seen as the greatest transgression of all. To them, gear placed on rappel had already undermined the main purpose of climbing a route.

It's fair to say that *Bachar-Yerian* was Bachar's response to this emergent top-down style. Assertive yet eloquent, the route posited that rock climbing shouldn't be reduced to something quantifiable, like chasing bigger numbers. The top-down approach missed something less tangible: the preservation of the adventure and boldness that many felt was the heart and soul of climbing. To Bachar and many others, upholding these ideals was most important. If any beginner with a drill could place bolts from the top down, the mental strength needed to climb ground-up would be lost in the rush to get more routes.

Initially sport climbing was both feared and loathed by trad climbers who were worried that every ground-up project would be bolted. Writer and provocateur John Sherman famously quipped, "Sport climbing is neither."

Sport climbers, on the other hand, found the traditional approach outdated, limiting, and unsuitable to every situation. Surely there was enough rock in the world for both top-down and ground-up styles. Besides, why make climbing an exercise in abstract ideals? Who cares *how* the bolts got there? Climbing should simply be about *climbing more.*

In Yosemite this clash of ideas played out between John Bachar and Ron Kauk, each assuming the personification of the opposing styles. Kauk, a gifted trad climber, also saw that sport climbing had a place in the greater world of rock climbing, and he bolted lines in Tuolumne and Yosemite Valley top-down.

There was much debate, including shouting matches and minor fisticuffs between members of the two climbers' respective factions. The conflict came to a climax in 1995 when Kauk rap-bolted Bachar's project *Diehard*, a thin, steep face

near the *Bachar-Yerian.* Kauk sent it and renamed the route *Peace* (5.13d), though the title hardly created much concord. Bachar believed that bolts ought to be placed on lead, and right up until 2009, when he died while free-soloing, Bachar faithfully stood by his ideals.

Outside of Yosemite's microcosm, sport climbing struggled to gain validity with just as much drama and conflict. Back at Smith in 1983, two weeks after sending *Watts Tots,* Alan Watts redpointed a stunning orange arête dubbed *Chain Reaction* (5.12c). The route was blank but enticing, and climbers had wondered whether it might be climbed in the future. One day, out of curiosity, Watts checked out the arête on rappel. He was thrilled to discover holds, and suddenly a sequence revealed itself.

It took Watts eight days to send *Chain Reaction.* After each attempt he'd remove (clean) his draws because ¬ he thought that the ascent wouldn't count unless he was placing his quickdraws on lead. Watts was stymied near the top of *Chain Reaction* by a pumpy clip right before the climactic "dyno," or leap, to the last hold of the route. On the day of his ascent, he realized that if he left the draws hanging, the last clip wouldn't be so sapping and the dyno would be more doable. He lowered to the ground, this time leaving the draws in place.

While Watts rested, he thought about it more and decided, after all, that he did need to place the draws on lead for the ascent to count. On his redpoint, Watts climbed up, took the draws off the bolts, clipped them to his harness, then unclipped them and placed them back on the very same bolts!

Watts' actions seem absurd to any sport climber these days, but it's often true that what was taboo yesterday is acceptable today and may not be tomorrow. Style and ethics in rock climbing will continue to shift as long as we continue to find difficult challenges for new climbers to solve using their own brands of skill, creativity, and vision.

As Watts made his way up the blank arête, a crowd gathered to watch the local star in action. When Watts clipped the last draw, made the dyno, and triumphantly latched the final jug, he knew that if something like *Chain Reaction* could go free, then the possibilities at Smith Rock for bolt-protected face climbing were unlimited.

"Almost overnight, the growing opposition to my style of climbing became just background noise," wrote Watts in Pat Ament's book *Wizards of Rock*. "I felt like a basketball player tuning out the raucous crowd, while sinking the game-winning shot. *Chain Reaction* became the poster child for a new style of climbing emerging in America."

In 1986 *Chain Reaction* appeared on the cover of *Mountain Magazine*, attracting the talents of the growing international sport-climbing community. That year the French climber J.B. Tribout visited Smith and managed to redpoint Watts' project, *To Bolt or Not To Be*, the first 5.14a on U.S. soil. (The year before, Wolfgang Güllich established the world's first 5.14a, *Punks in the Gym*, at Mount Arapiles, Australia).

BOLT WARS

Isolated sport routes began to appear in traditional zones throughout the country, at places like Red Rock Canyon (Red Rocks), Nevada; Joshua Tree, California; and Boulder and Eldorado canyons in Colorado.

Christian Griffith, the organically flamboyant icon of Boulder, not to mention a most talented rock climber, installed Eldorado's first rap-bolted route in 1985: *Paris Girl* (5.13a R). The bolts were chopped, then replaced. Then the first hanger was compromised with a deceptive cut—a potentially murderous act. It was replaced before anyone fell on the half-sawed bolt. Despite the melees, Griffith was undeterred and he produced two more significant Eldo sport climbs: *Desdichado* (5.13c), in 1985, one of the most spectacularly overhanging climbs ever achieved; and *Lakme* (5.13b), the unmistakable arête crowning the Redgarden Wall.

At the end of 1986 the American Alpine Club hosted the Great Debate, a gathering of the day's most influential climbers to discuss and define acceptable style and ethics. Henry Barber, Randy Vogel, Ron Kauk, Lynn Hill, John Bachar, Royal Robbins, John Gill, Layton Kor, Alan Watts, Todd Skinner, and Christian Griffith all attended. The issue was more complex than how, where, and if bolts should be placed—though these particular points certainly created the widest schisms. Even the Yosemite Decimal System was debated because it didn't account for how difficult it was to place gear versus the difficulty of clipping a preplaced bolt. How could a runout trad climb and a bolted face climb both be rated 5.11a?

In the end, like digging a ditch with a plastic spoon, the Great Debate didn't make a dent. Throughout the country the "Bolt Wars" continued as climbers decided that they'd do whatever they wanted. Bolts were chopped, more were drilled, and egos continued to collide.

From 1983 to roughly 1995, the American climbing scene struggled to define its identity amid its internal breakdown. Climbers were generally iconoclastic, operating at the fringes of society. Sport climbing, due to its accessibility and relative safeness, was bringing more people to the sport, which sent many xenophobic climbers into panics as they worried that climbing areas would soon be overrun and there'd be nowhere left to go.

Many early elite sport climbers garnered a reputation for being snarky and overly competitive. Some were just jerks. When they fell they threw "wobblers" (fits), and they had a propensity toward anorexia. The quintessence of such behavior was Jim Karn, America's best sport climber in the late 1980s. Not only was Karn the first American to win a World Cup—at La Riba, Spain, in 1988—but he climbed more 5.14s than anyone else, and quicker. Karn was ferociously driven to be the best. He eliminated all fat from his diet, which compromised his health and immune system, and left him as thin and tough as a strip of jerky. Karn's infamous fits were legendary, including throwing shoes and even smashing his competition trophies on the streets. During one onsight attempt at Rifle, Colorado, Karn blew the last move of *Sprayathon* (5.13c), causing him to wobble like he'd just stubbed his toe and bit his tongue at the same time. "I actually thought my head was going to explode," he reflected later. To make matters worse, sport climbers committed fashion suicide by dressing in gaudy Lycra tights. Some have claimed that Lycra was a rebellious statement against the canvas painters' pants worn by traditionalists, yet in retrospect, it can be accurately said that the Lycra era probably did more harm than good to the sport-climbing cause.

Despite these gawky growing pains, entire sport routes and crags began appearing everywhere, in Nevada at Red Rocks, Mount Potosi, and Mount Charleston; in California at Joshua Tree, Clark Mountain, and the Owens River Gorge; in Colorado at Boulder Canyon, Clear Creek Canyon, Shelf Road, and Rifle; in Arizona at the Virgin River Gorge; in Utah at American Fork, Black and Tan, and Gorilla Cliffs; in Kentucky at the Red River Gorge; in West Virginia at the New River Gorge; in Wyoming at Wild Iris; and in New Hampshire at Rumney.

Many climbers today take it for granted that there are so many cool places to go clip bolts, but few have a true appreciation for the amount of work and effort put in by these early pioneers, such as Alan Watts, Todd Skinner, Paul Piana, Alex Catlin, Jeff Jackson, Duane Raleigh, Kurt Smith, Chris Jones, Bill Ramsey, Porter Jarrard, Hugh Loffler, Boone Speed, Matt Samet, Jorge Visser, Randy Leavitt, and Scott Franklin, to name a few. Walls had to be found, trails built, and routes established, or "put up." Aside from the sheer expense of buying bolts (a single route can cost as much as $75) and driving to these often remote areas, drilling is back-breaking, core-sapping, brutal, thankless work. Then there's the task of actually sending the climb.

The labor yielded outstanding achievements. In 1987 Todd Skinner put up the now-forgotten classic *When Legends Die* (5.13a/b) at Hueco Tanks. The same year,

Fig. 1-2. Jeff Jackson, one of the sport's most active route developers in Texas and Mexico, is catching a belay from another prolific first ascentionist, Alex Catlin. (Photo © Boone Speed)

Jimmy Surrette, the Northeast's star free climber, put up *Edge of the World* (5.13c) on the airy arête capping Cathedral Ledge, New Hampshire. Scott Franklin repeated *To Bolt or Not To Be*, becoming the first American to climb 5.14a. In 1988 Duane Raleigh established the desperate, unrepeated *Colossus* (5.13d) in a now-closed granite quarry in Oklahoma. And from 1989 to 1994, Boone Speed, Jeff Pederson, Vince Adams, Tom Gilje, Scott Franklin, and Randy Leavitt were well at work on the Virgin River Gorge, establishing some of the country's longest limestone routes, such as Speed's *Fall of Man* (5.13b) in 1990, and *Route of All Evil* (5.14a) in 1994. At Clark Mountain, Leavitt climbed *Jumbo Pumping Hate* (5.14a) in 1995, and *Tusk* (5.14b) the next year.

In 1990 Lynn Hill became the first woman to climb 5.14a with her ascent of J.B. Tribout's *Mass Critique* at Cimai, France. This groundbreaking ascent was made all the more memorable by the fact that Tribout once famously said that no woman would ever be able to climb 5.14. Now, not only have dozens of women ticked the grade, but Josune Bereziartu, the Basque female powerhouse, has climbed *Bain de Sang* (5.14d) and *Bimbaluna* (5.14d/15a).

WILD ETHICS

Behind many outstanding feats were spates of dubious acts. Everyone was searching for the next best new sport crag—something that was accessible and steep, with holds and good rock. These traits, as simple as they seem, are actually quite rare, and many new sport crags tended to be on the *chossier* (rotten) side of the limestone spectrum. Establishing sport routes on the imperfect medium broadly called "choss" introduced a new gamut of ethical dilemmas.

How much rock was it acceptable to remove? Was it okay to use glue to secure holds that otherwise would break off? What about chipping? Though most agreed that manufacturing holds with a drill was wrong, what if it was done inconspicuously? What about "comfortizing," or making a preexisting sharp hold more comfortable to grab? It was argued that chipping could turn a route with one "impossible" move into a really enjoyable one. Some climbers proposed bolting artificial holds onto walls, holds that could be removed later when someone stronger came along. Though creative, most agreed that this was worse than a dumb idea.

Most agreed that gluing was bad and chipping was worse. Drilling holds into routes was "stealing from the future." Just because the first ascentionist couldn't do a move didn't give him a right to alter the rock.

Most first ascentionists weren't fazed by these opinions, which seemed to be formed in a vacuum. It was *their* route, *their* time, and *their* money. Some climbers spent hours sculpting holds that looked natural and painting the glue to camouflage it against the rock; others weren't so artistic. One sponsored climber, who was given bonuses for every 5.14 he climbed, drilled and chipped holds to create "new" routes that were really artificial link-ups into preexisting climbs. His sponsor wised up and dropped him.

Climbers were finding that with a little bit of the "lord's work," caves that had formerly been written off were transforming into really fun crags. Once again, perceptions were changing as new climbers challenged the old rules of the game. Climbers chipped and glued and cleaned—sometimes to make routes easier, sometimes to make them harder, and sometimes just to create a route where no holds had been. Most attempted to be discreet, but when things got out of hand the community stepped in and self-regulated.

These boundary-defining struggles were not dissimilar to what traditional climbing went through in the 1970s when it shifted toward an ethic of using "clean" protection, not pitons, that wouldn't scar the rock. Just as pitons gave Yosemite its most popular 5.10a, *201*

Crack (unintentionally "manufactured" by piton scars), chipping, aggressive cleaning, and gluing gave sport climbing some of its most popular (and detested) routes. This give, take, and debate created the characteristics and flavors of many crags and climbs.

The Smith route *Just Do It* (5.14c)—America's first 5.14c, sent by J.B. Tribout and bolted by Alan Watts—suffered from climbers' dubious ethics. The crux originally involved a long, difficult pull off a single-finger pocket, or "mono." When Tribout showed up to work the line, the mono "somehow" became a two-finger slot. Scott Franklin, another route suitor, was pissed off by the "improvement" and filled

the hold with Sika glue to restore its original size. Footholds were also reinforced and made larger with Sika. Eventually another climber found that the mono move could be skipped entirely by grabbing the glued footholds—beta that has since become the approved sequence.

One hilarious anecdote is the creation of Smith Rock's *Scarface* (5.14a). Originally, a hollow, table-sized flake of rock halfway up this route made the climbing easier. Deciding the flake had to go, Scott Franklin taped M-80s behind it, lit them, and rapped off quickly. When the dust settled, Franklin was dismayed to see the flake perfectly intact. The next day he enlisted the help of Mark Twight and Randy Rackliff, alpinists who were passing through Smith on their way home from Alaska, to bash away at it, first with ice hammers and then with sledgehammers. The flake finally crumbled, leaving a three-finger pocket in its place and the namesake white scar on the face.

In the early 1990s these controversial tactics were most rampantly used in the Hell Cave of American Fork, Utah, as well as at Mount Charleston and Mount Potosi, both outside of Las Vegas, Nevada. Today, these places are frequented mostly by locals who appreciate the convenience of a nearby outdoor workout; they are no longer the destinations they once were because the poor ethics and lame tactics have left the climbs short on legacy.

It would be unfair, however, not to acknowledge how chipping routes has helped raise standards. The unmatched density of 5.14 climbers in Spain's Basque region is largely due to the many manufactured and chipped "training" routes in the area. When properly done, chipping and gluing have resulted in popular fitness-building climbs such as Rifle's *Living in Fear* (5.13d).

One excellent example of ethical integrity in action is the story of Randy Leavitt's old project on Clark Mountain. When he realized the route was "all there" but way above his abilities, he left the route alone for the next generation instead of chipping holds to make it easier for him. More than fifteen years later it took an epic campaign by Chris Sharma to send *Jumbo Love* (5.15b), one of the hardest free climbs in the world. It's exactly this sort of precedent that will, and should, shape the future of the sport.

THE NEXT GENERATION

By the mid 1990s sport climbing was introduced to its first "next generation" of athletes—young, preternatural climbers who began climbing in gyms on youth competition teams. It felt as though not just sport climbing but climbing in general was beginning to veer in a new direction.

At nine years old in 1994, Chris Lindner sent his first 5.13a and became the youngest American to tick the grade. In 1995 Katie Brown, at fourteen, won the Junior World Cup in France. In 1996, Sharma, 14, bolted his first route, *Übermensch* (5.13d), at Pinnacles National Monument, California. When he turned 15, Sharma blew the community away by sending seven 5.14s in a three-week trip. In 1997, at 16, Sharma sent *Necessary Evil* (5.14c) at the Virgin River Gorge (VRG), establishing the hardest route in America.

Bill Ramsey, a philosophy professor who has been sport climbing since it first kicked off at Smith—and who contributed such 5.14a routes as *Omaha Beach* and *Transworld Depravity* at the Red River Gorge in the early 1990s—puts the shift in perspective:

"In the mid-'90s there were a number of climbers vying for top dog and trying to become, in some way, professional climbers. Some of them took themselves and their climbing very seriously, and this sometimes led to behavior that was, let's say, a bit embarrassing—people acting like jerks to lesser climbers, fighting for attention and sponsorships, that sort of thing. Anyhow, when the next generation came along it seemed like overnight everything changed. I'm thinking of people like Chris Sharma, Dave Hume, Katie Brown, Dave Graham, Tommy Caldwell, Beth Rodden, Ethan Pringle. First, this new crop was so much stronger that they demolished any pretense among the older guard that one of *them* might be the best. The youngsters were just great kids, friendly to everyone, with little or no ego. It was ironic that they received the fanfare and support others had been seeking, but it seemed like they couldn't care less. They just wanted to go climbing all the time. In my view, the sport took a turn for the better."

What separated these climbers from those of the earlier generations is that

Fig 1-1. Dave Graham, one of the next generation's most technically gifted free climbers, took two tries to send this incredible 55-metre line, Los Humilides pa Caasa (5.14b), Olina, Spain. (Photo © Keith Ladzinski)

they weren't products of any stylistic or ethical antagonisms. They were just psyched on free climbing as hard as they could—whether on boulders, sport routes, or in comps, it didn't really matter. It was all seen as part of one thing.

Chris Sharma recalls his first trip to Céüse, at age 16. "I walked up the hill, saw *Realization*, and that was the first thing I got on. No warming up...nothing." It took Sharma three more trips over the next four years before he was actually capable of doing the route. But in 2001, at age 20, Sharma sent *Realization*, the benchmark 5.15a and one of the world's first.

It was the distinct *lack of ego* in these prodigies, despite their achievements, that steered sport climbing in a direction for it to flourish.

Just as ideas and preconceptions about

difficulty had taken a swing, so had attitudes toward chipping and gluing. Though they were still climbing on the chipped routes of yesterday, taking chisel to rock was unheard of among this next generation. Dave Graham, perhaps the most technically gifted free climber of this generation, even went as far as saying that chipped routes were "easy" . . . and he continues to prove it by onsighting most chipped routes regardless of grade.

At Rumney, Graham, along with his two friends Joe Kinder and Luke Parady, cleaned up. At 16, Graham single-handedly gave the Waimea Wall the distinction of having the highest concentration of 5.14s in the country, sending routes like *Jaws* (5.14b), *China Beach* (5.14b), and *Livin' Astro* (5.14c).

The Graham-Parady-Kinder trio is one of the most emblematic examples of the new shift in attitude toward sport and style. The trio shared a matchless passion for climbing, pushing each other to excel in competitive yet positive ways. For example, after meeting Graham, Kinder went from climbing 5.13b to 5.14b in six months.

In the late 1990s and early 2000s, bouldering also became an important focus for this emergent clan. The Bouldering Boom, as it came to be called, produced such iconic lines as Sharma's *Mandala* (V12) and Graham's *Specter* (V13), both in Bishop, California. Climbers who dedicated years to bouldering revealed that it's possible to combine truly hard boulder problems with the endurance of long routes. In 2006, in Ticino, Switzerland, Graham established

Coup de Grace (5.15a), which he called "the world's first hybrid route," meaning that the climb combines multiple V12 power cruxes with the stamina of a sport climb.

The next, *next* generation took it to an even higher level. Shortly after the Czech prodigy Adam Ondra turned 15, he climbed two 5.15a routes in one week during a break from high school. Ondra's tally in 2008 alone was twenty-eight 5.14b routes (three of them onsight), twenty-three 5.14c routes, nine 5.14d routes, and two 5.15a routes. It's no exaggeration to say Ondra and his peers have a bright future ahead of them.

Many accomplished sport climbers such as Sonnie Trotter, Alex Honnold, and Ethan Pringle, and boulderer/comp climbers such as Matt Wilder and Kevin Jorgeson, have brought their free-climbing skills to the realm of trad. In his first year of placing gear Ethan Pringle climbed over a dozen 5.13d-and-harder trad climbs such as *The Path* (5.14a R) and *Cobra Crack* (5.14b/c), both climbs first sent by Sonnie Trotter. During a three-month climbing stint, Alex Honnold onsighted the infamous gritstone route *Gaia* (E8, or 5.12+ R/X), free climbed El Capitan via the route *El Niño* (5.13c), and redpointed a handful of sport climbs rated 5.14b. It's interesting to see how sport climbing, originally the antithetical progeny of trad climbing, is now having the largest (and most positive) influence on the thing it tried so hard to rebel against.

While trad climbing will surely continue to benefit from sport-honed skills and techniques, it is sport climbing itself that arguably has the brightest future. As of 2009 sport climbers are just beginning to realize that really long single-pitch routes can be combined with truly hard moves. These modern routes are going to look like Sharma's *Jumbo Love* (5.15b), a 250-foot masterpiece of limestone architecture at Clark Mountain.

In fact it's happening not just among the elites but at everyday crags around the country. Seventy- and 80-meter ropes have replaced 50- and 60-meter ones. Modern sport climbers skip bolts and take big falls, knowing the protection is good and their belayers know how to give soft catches. With levels of fitness and skill that only twenty years ago were possessed by just a few top athletes, the new-generation climbers are realizing how feasible it is for "regular" people to redpoint long, brilliant sport routes.

The rise in standards is great, but the best change of all is the friendly social scene. To call yourself a sport climber nowadays is to enter a global network of friendships that reconnect when conditions are good.

As standards rise, hopefully the lessons of our dramatic history will not be lost: nothing is impossible, and respect—for the rock, for the experience, and for each other—is ultimately what's most important.

CHAPTER 2

Free climbing often means twisting and turning your body into some of the most outrageous positions, as demonstrated by Kleman Becan on a 5.13c in Spain. (Photo © Keith Ladzinski)

Free Yourself With Great Climbing Technique

Free climbing is one of the most liberating, and challenging, activities you'll ever do. Free climbing is as natural to us as running. Perhaps that explains its primal thrill, the feeling that this is something we were always meant to do, which reveals itself on the good days when you're light, in control, and on the loose.

Climbing technique comes down to linking basic foot, hand, and body positions into one flowing, upward motion. The basic positions are easily outlined, but their permutations are infinite. No text could ever do justice to the actual experience of getting out and going up. But this chapter will give some tips for starting out, and advice for climbing well, no matter what your ability.

WHAT IS "GOOD" TECHNIQUE?

Technically, any technique that gets you to the top of a climb is good.

When Chris Sharma busted onto the scene as a teenager, the old guard derived endless satisfaction from criticizing him for having bad technique. He had "bad footwork," they said, because he rarely had both feet on the wall at the same time (the other was usually kicked out), which went against old concepts of always maintaining three points of contact.

Actually, Sharma's bounding, dynamic movement was a display of total efficiency for him. In fact his technique was stylistically ahead of its time, breaking many old notions of what had formerly been considered good technique. On closer inspection, climbers realized that kicking his foot away from the wall on certain dynamic moves actually provided him stability in the same way that a lashing cheetah's tail creates the balance needed to maneuver at high speeds. Sharma also showed that sometimes the most efficient technique for surpassing difficulties is to simply jump for the next hold!

This is not to say that everyone should climb like Sharma (though that would certainly help), but to point out that each body is different. Sharma is tall and powerful, and so making big, powerful moves fits him. Some climbers have more endurance, and will do better by hanging on and climbing slowly and steadily. It's insanely cool that fifty climbers can climb one route in fifty different ways.

At some point, however, when the moves get hard, everyone (even Sharma) must resort to sound climbing fundamentals. Mastering the ground rules should always be your number-one goal. Learning technique should trump worrying about training regimens or ticking the next highest grade. I mention this because, in my experience, with so many excellent indoor climbing facilities around, and a culture that encourages higher numbers over the quality of skill, it has become increasingly common for newcomers to get *too strong, too quickly*. In other words, beginners tend to rely on big forearms to get up 5.11 and 5.12 routes in the gym, where you can get away with that sort of thing, but outside

they lack the technique needed to climb routes of the same grade.

This is problematic for a couple of reasons: first and most obviously, you need to learn great technique if you want to become a great climber. Second, racing up through the grades due to strength rather than technique creates a false sense of ability that encourages climbers to get on hard, crimpy routes before their tendons are really ready for it. While the musculature may be there, building up tendon resilience takes a long time—sometimes three years or more. This is why so many new climbers pop finger tendons and have bad elbow pain in their first three years of climbing, while more seasoned climbers (who take care of their bodies) don't.

To learn good technique you need humility and patience, because proficiency and mastery of climbing technique are best gleaned by spending a lot of time on easier routes. Dani Andrada, one of the best climbers in the world, redpointed fifty 5.13b routes before he even considered getting on a 5.13c. While those grades are admittedly elite, the lesson still applies: take the time needed to master the easier grades before moving on. Did you redpoint fifty 5.11ds before even trying a 5.12a?

There are five fundamentals of good climbing technique:

1) **Create balance.** Stand up straight and spread your weight evenly between both feet. Your two straight legs supply an equal and opposite force to gravity's, which prevents you from crumpling

Fig. 2-1. Achieving balance means creating harmony between the hand and footholds with clever body positions. Here the climber "flags" his right leg underneath the left to create a stable position that allows him to clip a quickdraw.

over. Though we're accustomed to it, creating this balance requires a very specific pose and the energy to maintain its form. This is what it feels like to be in balance—you're in a pose, using energy, albeit as little as possible, to hold it. The vertical realm, however, presents many more dimensions than the flat ground, and achieving balance up on a route is rarely as simple as standing on two feet.

In rock climbing, balance involves grabbing holds with your hands, placing your feet on footholds, and allowing your torso to twist naturally around these points of contact so you can move up (or over) to the next hold. Balance in climbing means doing whatever is necessary to transfer your weight through your feet (as you do when standing). It may seem crazy, but in the multidimensional world of rock climbing this could even mean doing a kneebar above your head and rotating your torso around it!

Balance is achieved through a harmony of two or three hand- or footholds at once. Good balance is worthless, however, unless it sets your body up to make the next move.

Think about that. Often climbers (particularly men with a high level of preexisting strength) focus so much on getting to the next hold that they don't bother setting up their balance first. The climber sees the next grip and dives for it—and invariably one leg swings away from the wall, pulling him off balance.

Another common error beginners make is trying to move more than one limb at the same time. You will be out of balance if you try to grab the next handhold before you've completely set your foot.

So remember: *balance first, move second.*

And as important as it is to know what it feels like to be in balance, it's equally important to know what it feels like to be out of balance, ideally so you can fix it on the spot. Often it's a subtle sensation in your lower abdomen, where your center of gravity is. Being out of balance feels like your core is *peeling* away from you.

It is also sometimes described as a feeling of *not being able to move*. Beginners commonly (and mistakenly) dismiss this sensation as not being strong enough. In some cases that might be true, but most of the time a subtle (or extreme) shift in body position will put you in balance and set you up perfectly to make that next move.

Finally, there's the element of anticipation. For example, you must be able to anticipate whether taking your left hand off the wall will be okay or if it will send you off kilter. When a climber moves a limb and unexpectedly peels away from the wall, it's called "barn-dooring." Learning to anticipate these forces and respond to them through intuitive body positions is what being in balance is all about.

2) Use your feet. In rock climbing your feet have only two jobs: 1) to take weight off of your arms, and 2) to drive your body upward.

Feet take weight off your arms when you allow yourself to really stand on them. Because most footholds are no bigger than a pencil eraser, this technique can be difficult to learn unless you have a background in ballet, where standing on your toes is par for the course.

There's a big difference between sloppily plopping your foot down onto a hold and placing it with precision. Always try to place your feet "silently."

The most common mistake beginners make is kicking their foot at a hold or kicking the wall just above the foothold, and letting their foot scrape down the wall until it crash-lands onto the edge. Imagine that footholds are receivers, you're the quarterback, and your toe is the ball. Aim to hit your target quickly and accurately on your first try.

The orientation of your foot on a foothold is key. Eighty percent of your body—everything from your chest down to your feet—connects to the rock through your toes. How you place your feet, and where, makes all the difference.

Pay special attention to your knees, hips, and core, and their relation to your feet. On steeper routes (anything steeper than 85 degrees vertical), you want your hips as close to the wall as possible. The closer you can get one hip (or sometimes both) to the rock, the more weight you

will be able to transfer onto your feet, which means less weight on your arms.

When your hips are close to the wall, your knee will be pointing out to the side. This means your thigh (inner or outer, depending on which way your foot is facing) is nearly flush to the wall.

On less-steep faces, also called "slabs," keep your weight over your feet, fully balanced. This may mean moving your hips out away from the wall, almost like a standing version of the yoga pose "downward dog."

Beginners hug the rock and/or grope too high for out-of-reach holds, making it hard to see and use their feet. Place your feet first, then reach for a handhold. If a handhold seems too far away, the answer will *always, always* be to change something about your feet.

Footholds require precision. As an exercise, get down and inspect footholds. Start looking for the best edge, and then the best part of that edge. With experience, spotting good footholds will become second nature. On many well-traveled routes, keep an eye out for the black rubber scuff marks. These indicate footholds other climbers have used and offer clues to deciphering the proven sequence.

Vertical to less-steep routes fatigue toes and feet. Just as you will focus on relaxing your hand's grip, it may be equally important to relax your toes. Let

Fig. 2-2. Hanging from straight arms is most efficient. Here, Whitney Boland warms up on Chainsaw Massacre *(5.12a), Red River Gorge, Kentucky* (Photo © Keith Ladzinski)

the shoe do the work and don't press too hard with your toes. If you feel your toes cramping up, look for a big edge and place your heel on it so you are standing on that heel, thus giving your toes a reprieve.

3) **Relax your grip.** While your feet play the biggest role in taking weight off of your arms, it's also important to learn how to relax your arms, too.

Hang from *straight arms*. By relaxing the shoulders, forearms, and back muscles you can transfer your weight onto your skeletal system. Hang from your bones! With your arms straight, sink down, *not out*—the more you come away from the wall, the more weight you put on your arms. This usually means you will need to turn your hip/knee out from the wall even more to make room for yourself to get low. Drop your collar bone so it sinks down in relation to your shoulder. Hanging from your skeleton almost feels as if your shoulder disengages from its socket a bit.

Of course, it would be impossible to climb if you kept your arms straight the whole time. You have to bend them and flex your muscles to pull up to the next hold. But instead of initiating this motion by flexing your lats, *press down on your feet first*.

Always initiate any upward movement with your lower limbs. Only after the upward movement has been initiated with the legs should you begin to flex your arms.

Master this technique by climbing easy routes in the gym. Try to climb them using your arms only for balance; drive yourself up the wall with strategic footwork and leg strength.

Also relax your hands' grip. Now relax it some more. You want to be so relaxed that if you let go of the hold any more, you would fall off. It takes about a year (and usually longer) of climbing to gain the finger and muscle awareness needed to let go this much while still hanging on, not to mention fully integrating it into your climbing style.

Bouldering is the complete opposite. Boulder problems are short and the moves are hard and powerful. You won't get pumped on a short boulder problem, so you may as well crush every single grip in order to reach the top.

Sport climbing is a more complex discipline because you will need to strategically employ the intensity of that bouldering grip to surpass the hard moves while simultaneously knowing when to relax and ease off. In some cases you may be crushing a hold with your left hand while trying to keep the right hand relaxed.

Think of your grip strength like a manual transmission—redlining the car will cause you to run out of gas quicker. Sometimes you need to downshift to accelerate through a difficult section, but for the most part you want to keep the RPMs low to conserve fuel.

Knowing when and how hard to

punch it, and when to ease off, is the mark of a good route climber.

4) **Be efficient.** Don't spend a lot of energy matching on a hold when you could simply cross through to the next hold. Don't switch your feet back and forth, making five moves when you could reach the same spot with one or two.

Efficiency is best learned experimenting on a route you are trying to redpoint. Try the same move in two or three different ways. Does one way feel easier than the other? Figure out why. You are a student of the rock; take every opportunity to learn.

When practicing any section of a route, always climb into the sequence you want to work on. One common error most climbers make is, after falling, starting on the high hold in a different body position than the one they will be in after climbing up from lower holds. By committing this error they work out a sequence using a body position that isn't true to the route's real sequence. Practice moves by starting two or three holds down from the fall point, and climbing up into the troublesome sequence.

Each route has its own rhythm, and your goal is to sync yourself with that beat. There is great efficiency in momentum, letting yourself swing up to the next hold with ease. Sometimes the rhythm isn't that fast, such as on a delicate slab. There's still a beat, albeit a slower, steadier one. The best way to get into the rhythm is to climb on a top

rope that's not running through any quickdraws—except, of course, the anchor ones. Without having to stop to clip or unclip, you can just experience the pure movement of an entire pitch. Let yourself *flow* up it.

Some moves are dynamic, while others are best executed statically. Dynamic moves require power, while static moves require pure strength—two different but related things. Strength is the maximum load a single contracted muscle can support. Power means tapping into the strength of one or more muscle groups to complete a movement in as short a period of time as possible. Pure strength involves "locking off" on a hold and holding that position. Power means the speed at which you can exert that strength—instead of "locking off" to reach up to the next hold, you *burst* up to it. Almost all routes will be most efficiently climbed using a combination of both static and dynamic moves.

The more routes you climb, and the more moves you learn, the more efficient you will become. Most beginners start out with the adroitness needed to climb a ladder: right hand up, left foot up; left hand up, right foot up; repeat. Over the course of thousands of routes on many different types of rock, you will steadily fill your reservoir of climbing moves and body positions. As the reservoir gets bigger, you will find yourself climbing more efficiently, and doing harder routes quicker and more easily.

Fig. 2-3. Isaac Caldiero making a dynamic "deadpoint" on a 5.13 at Acephale, Bow Valley, Canada (Photo © Keith Ladzinski)

5) Learn how to rest and how to shake out. On a sport climb, resting is often *the* definitive difference between sending and falling. There's technique to resting, but to a large degree it's physical. The physical side of resting is called "recovery," which is the measure of how quickly and how fully you can regain the strength and stamina to continue climbing.

Often there are definitive rests on most climbs—places that, for one reason or another, allow you to remain in one place, catch your breath, get the lactic acid out of your forearms, and recharge your batteries. A rest may be anything from a ledge that gives you a nice comfortable stance (or seat), to a place to stem, to a nice jug to hang from. It could also be a hold that is small and pumpy, but compared to all the other holds on the route it's the best one. Sometimes rests are compromises—maybe your forearms are getting a reprieve, but your legs and feet are maintaining a strenuous position, tiring them out.

As your forearms become pumped you'll need to shake them out. Bring your arm down to your side and shake your whole arm softly but vigorously for two or three seconds. Don't shake it too crazily. After that two-second shake, let your arm hang limp. Open and close your fist to help pump blood through your veins. Take a deep breath in, then breathe out just as deeply. As you breathe out, imagine all the tension, pain, and anxiety dissipating. The goal is to bring freshness, relaxation, and stillness to each joint and every muscle fiber. For just a moment, be still and focused.

Switch your hands on the resting hold, and repeat the sequence with your other hand. Continue switching your hands back and forth, shaking each one out. With each shake, picture your battery slowly recharging.

Also, mix it up. Instead of bringing your arm down to the side to shake it out, leave it up in the air and shake with your hand over your head. Shaking out your arm above your head uses gravity to flush blood out of your swollen forearms. The faster you can get the blood to circulate through your forearm, the faster your body will begin to metabolize the lactic acid that is causing your arm to ache.

If your strength isn't coming back at all, you may need to abandon the "rest" and just keep going. You will likely fall, but there's a chance you could make it to a better rest.

If you find yourself unable to recover on even the largest holds, you'll need to train your muscles. Next time you reach a resting hold and you're pumped, just stay there, holding on as long as you can. Do this on as many routes as you can. After about three weeks of training to improve your recovery—simply hanging on a hold, totally pumped, shaking out and trying to get it back—you should begin to notice improvement. If you're still not improving, take a week off from

Fig. 2-4. Spanish climber Berta Martin shakes out on a 5.13d in Rodellar, Spain, by jamming her leg into a tufa and hanging from a straight arm. (Photo © Keith Ladzinski)

climbing and do some trail running.

Another shaking trick is to give a very quick shake in between grabbing holds. As you move your hand from one hold to the next one, give it a quick shake. You don't get much back from this technique, but you get a little. Over the course of an entire route, this can add up.

Ultimately, your mental and technical ability to find rests on holds, coupled with your physical ability to recover, is going to be a deciding factor in whether you send or fall.

FOOTWORK

Edging. Edges are flat or semi-flat features/ridges/ripples in the rock, and edging means standing on edges using the outer

Fig. 2-6. Get as much shoe rubber on the rock as possible when smearing; keep the heels low.

Fig. 2-5. Classic edging with the left toe

rim of your rock shoe, the part beneath your toes. Most of the time you edge with your big toe (figure 2-5), but when you stand on the outer edge of your shoe, it's called "outside edging" or "backstepping."

Smearing. A smear is a dishlike surface that you "paste" your toes onto. Smears aren't really holds per se, just surfaces that allow you to use the friction of your shoe rubber to stand up on them. Smearing is harder than edging because it feels as if you aren't standing on anything at all.

Flexing your ankle and lowering your heel often gives you more rubber-to-rock contact (figure 2-6). Try to maintain that constant angle of foot flex as you stand up, otherwise you might slide off the hold. The more you can weight a smear, the more rubber you will get on the rock.

Hooking. There are two types of hooks: heel hooks and toe hooks. Heel hooks are excellent ways to pull your weight up, over, or around a steep feature. To heel hook, place your heel on a surface, usually an edge level with your upper body, and pull down on it with your hamstring (figure 2-7). When standing on an edge doesn't work, look around for a hidden heel hook, as they can create balance. A vertical feature that's facing away from you would be impossible

Fig 2-7. Heel hooks help take the weight off your arms, but they are also used to surmount steep features.

to edge on, but you might be able to heel hook it. Well-fitting shoes are needed here.

Toe hooking is less common but definitely useful, especially on overhanging terrain or when there aren't any footholds to push down on. Dave Graham has mastered this technique, and using his crazy toe-hooking skills he can keep his feet on the rock even when there seem to be no footholds at all. To toe hook, wrap the top of your foot around a corner, above a lip, or in an "undercling" position.

Toe hooks really shine on overhangs. One variation of the toe hook is a move called the "bicycle," where you toe down on a feature with one foot while simultaneously opposing that force in the opposite direction with a slick toe hook. A bicycle may be just the vehicle you need to get through roofs or steep overhangs.

Toeing down. As the terrain gets steeper you'll want to start toeing down on footholds. This looks exactly like edging, only the action of your toe is more pronounced. Imagine your big toe as a claw that wants to actually dig into a foothold and wrap around the inside of it. Shoes with softer rubber and a downturned last are best here. While toeing down, pull with your hamstring and use the strength of your hip—this motion simultaneously sucks your hip and core closer to the wall.

HANDHOLDS

Jugs. These are the biggest, best holds around, and they come in all shapes and varieties. Always hold jugs using as *little* energy as possible. Try holding on using only the friction of your skin. Most importantly, learn how to rest on jugs. Can you fit two hands onto a single jug, taking turns hanging by one hand while shaking the other out? Look for jugs near bolts—often, routes have been equipped so that the hardware is near the best holds.

Crimps. Crimps, or crimpers, are fingertip-sized edges that you'll use in one of three hand positions: full-crimp, half-crimp, and open-hand.

For the full-crimp, place your fingers on an edge, furling them such that your first knuckles become concave; now wrap your thumb on top of the nails of your index finger and middle finger (figure 2-8). This is the most powerful position for tiny holds, but also the most injury-prone as it places

Fig. 2-8. Full-crimp

high stress on finger tendons.

The half-crimp is just like the full-crimp only it doesn't incorporate the thumb. You expend less energy in a half-crimp position than a full-crimp.

The open-hand crimp is reserved for easier holds that you hang onto with relaxed (unfurled) fingers (figure 2-9). Practice open-hand crimping as much as possible because this builds forearm muscles and contact strength better than the other two positions, which strain tendons and cause tennis elbow. Open-hand crimping also builds the muscles needed to hang onto slopers and pockets.

If crimping is hurting your fingers' tendons, take a break from the full- and half-crimp. Use only the open-hand crimp, unless that hurts, too. Icing your fingers for fifteen minutes after a day of climbing will help prevent injury. If your tendons hurt, *don't take ibuprofen* before climbing! Climbing on painkillers masks the sensation telling us to stop. I know at least a few climbers whose careers have ended when their already injured tendons popped in an ibuprofen-fueled climbing binge.

Pockets. Pockets are holes in a rock face that, depending on their size, accept from one to three fingers (figure 2-10). Grab pockets with straight, unfurled fingers. Sometimes pockets are large enough to crimp. Search around for the sweet spot, which could be hidden toward the back of the pocket, the side, or even the top. Get as many fingers as possible in there—this could mean stacking your fingers by placing your middle finger on top of your index finger. One-finger pockets are called "monos." A four-finger pocket is called a "slot."

Pinches. This hold is the most "evolved" as it incorporates the thing that separates us from all animals except primates: the opposable thumb. The most classic pinch is a vertical protrusion in the rock, such as a "tufa," that you can squeeze/pinch with your fingers (figure 2-11). Pinches, however, can be angled in any direction, so be open-minded. Look for thumb indentations

Fig. 2-9. Open-hand

Fig. 2-10. Two-finger pocket

Fig. 2-11. Pinch grip

around the corner from a crimper or pocket that will turn the hold into a nice pinch.

Underclings and side pulls. These can be like jugs, edges, or crimpers, only they face in a different direction and are therefore given different names. An undercling is a hold that you grab with your palm facing up toward the sky. Underclings work different muscles than regular down-pulling holds, the biceps in particular.

As the name implies, a side pull is a hold you grab from the side. It may seem strange that a hold you pull from the *side* would help you move *up*. Again, it's all about proper body position. Grabbing two side pulls may provide the equal and opposite force needed to keep balanced, step your feet up high, and subsequently reach above to the next hold. Often you will counter the force of a single side pull by backstepping

Fig. 2-12. Slopers—note the straight arms under the hands and close to the wall.

Fig. 2-13. Pull out left on this "reverse side pull," also called a gaston.

(using the outside edge of) the foot on the opposite side of your body. Maintain relaxation on the side pull, leaning away from the hold with a straight arm.

Slopers. A bald, often convex feature that slants away from the wall at a (usually poor) angle is a sloper. You don't really "grab" slopers, but simply put your entire palm on it and rely on the friction between your hand and the rock to keep you on the wall. Slopers are surprisingly difficult to use, owing to their complexity and the technique they demand. Even more so than most holds, good body position is *imperative* to hanging on slopers. In general you want to *stay low* on the hold by keeping your elbow pointing directly down toward the ground—when your elbow begins to come up and away from the wall (called "chicken winging"), there will be less friction between your hand and the rock.

Feel around for the best part—maybe you'll find an indentation that will provide your fingertips with an extra bit of purchase. Keep your fingers close and let them work together—like the front line of an infantry, there's strength in numbers here.

Gastons. The gaston is a hold/move named after the French mountain guide Gaston Rébuffat. It can best be described as a "reverse side pull," or an edge facing the wrong way. Hold a gaston by positioning your hand on it such that your pinkie is higher than your thumb, and your elbow is cocked up/out to the side. If a gaston feels unusable, try pressing into it by using a high foot on the opposite side of your body from the gaston.

BODY POSITIONS AND MOVEMENT

Matching. This simply means placing both hands, or both feet, on the same hold. Matching hands on a big hold is relatively simple. Matching a smaller hold is more complicated, and it may require taking one finger off in order to make room for the incoming hand. Matching hands can be strenuous unless the hold is a jug. In general, the shorter you are the more matching you will find yourself doing.

Matching feet is an excellent, common, and useful technique that you'll do on just about every route you climb. To match your feet, place the toe of your incoming foot *directly* above the toe of the foot on the hold. Now, as smoothly as you can, hop the lower foot off the hold, and stab the new foot down in its place.

Occasionally, briefly matching a hold allows you to break up a long pull. Pause on the hold and continue pulling up to gain the next one. This technique is also called "using an intermediate," which is a hold that's not good enough to use but which gives you something to pause on before continuing to a better hold.

Crossover/crossunder. A crossing move involves diving one arm over or under the other in order to gain a handhold. A crossing move that works will leave the other arm enough room to make the next move. A crossing move for your feet is called "walking your feet through." A well-executed crossing move is one of the most efficient techniques there is in free

Fig. 2-14. With legs bridged between two planes of a dihedral, Jessa Younker cops a stem in Mill Creek, Utah. (Photo © David Clifford)

climbing—look to cross your feet or hands instead of matching. The photo that opens this chapter shows a crossover.

High-stepping. Place the inside edge of your shoe on a high foothold and "rock on to it." In other words, shift your weight over onto the foot, so that your center of gravity (located in your core) is directly over that foot. Efficient, clean, beautiful.

Stemming. This technique involves smearing or edging your feet against two opposing planes of rock, making your body look like an upside-down Y. You use your legs to create a stable and balanced platform, thereby taking most (or all) of the weight off your arms. Most people think of stemming as a technique used in "open books," otherwise called "dihedrals," and they would be right. However, a good sport climber will be able to stem between any two footholds that acutely jut out from the plane of the wall. Always look to cop a stem whenever possible, especially as you read the next sequence. But think of efficiency, too. Will the energy it takes to get into the perfect stem be worth it? Will you get enough of a rest, or will it be more strenuous than restful?

Liebacking. The lieback creates balance through opposition: You pull on a side, pull in one direction, and find balance by pushing your feet against the wall in the opposite direction. When liebacking, shuffle your hands up, keeping your arms straight and your feet low. The higher your feet are, the more strenuous the lieback is. However,

the smoother and steeper the rock, the higher your feet must go. Find a rhythm when liebacking—sometimes it's best not to stop until you reach a stem or a jug.

Manteling. This involves pressing down on a section of rock, using your shoulder and tricep muscles to push your body up as if you're getting out of a swimming pool. The mantel is generally used to surmount a ledge, large or small, where there are no handholds above to help pull you up. This technique requires push-up strength, balance, and the flexibility to match your foot and hand.

Drop knee. Here's a fancy way to get your hips close to the wall and utilize footholds that are otherwise unusable. To drop knee, place the outside edge of your foot onto a hold, and swing your knee downward. (Check out the photo that opens this chapter to see an extreme drop knee.) Drop knees are great ways to get your weight close to the wall on overhanging climbs. Be careful: drop knees are strenuous and may cause injury to some patellae. If you have bad knees that prevent drop-kneeing, take an Iyengar yoga class or two (or a hundred). Iyengar is a type of yoga that uses props to put you into restorative positions that bring flexibility and motion to joints and muscles.

Kneebar. Bridge the lower half of your leg, from your toe to your knee, between two planes of rock. It's as if the lower half of your leg becomes a prop holding the rock in place. Place your foot on the foothold,

Fig. 2-15. Patrick Pharo liebacks a sidepull by pushing with his feet and pulling with his left arm.

Fig. 2-16. Sometimes, a good kneebar will let you take your hands off the wall, even in the middle of an overhanging roof. (Photo © Marni Mattner)

and place your knee against the opposing rock surface you want to kneebar against. Now press down with your toe and push the top of your knee into the rock, flexing your calf muscle *hard*. Kneebars come in all varieties of usefulness. Sometimes a kneebar is so bad it is barely useful—in this case it would be called a "knee scum." Other times kneebars are so good you can take your hands off the wall.

If you're lucky enough to find a kneebar that lets you take your hands off the wall on an overhanging rock climb, just hang upside-down. Don't sit there, flexing your core muscles in a sit-up position. Just let it go: relax your abs, your face muscles, and your back. Shake out by alternately letting your arms hang down above your head and pointing them up to the sky (figure 2-16).

Dyno/deadpoint. Dynamic moves use momentum to create efficiency through a free-climbing sequence. A "dyno" is the most dynamic move there is in climbing, and it involves literally jumping for a hold and then latching it, while the feet swing free. There are also two-handed dynos, when a climber jumps for a hold and grabs it with both hands at once.

A deadpoint is less dynamic than a dyno, but often more efficient than a *static* pull. Deadpointing (figure 2-3) is just like dynoing, only your feet don't cut away from the wall. Set your feet on good footholds and push really hard while simultaneously pulling down with one arm. The other hand goes for the far-away hold. Time the moment your body hits that weightless "deadpoint," the apex of the upward reach, with the instant you contact the hold. You need good concentration and coordination to successfully stick deadpoints. Focus like a laser beam during the entire range of motion; don't take your eye off the hold you're going for. Be positive and don't hesitate. Committing to a dynamic move is sometimes harder than actually doing it.

CHAPTER 3

Sonnie Trotter on the first ascent of The Mistress (5.13b), Yamnuska, Canada (Photo © Keith Ladzinski)

Gear You Need: How to Choose It, Use It, and Keep It Safe

One of the great joys of sport climbing is that it doesn't require a whole lot of gear. Well, that's only partially true. At a bare minimum, you need a harness, rope, belay device, climbing shoes, chalk, chalkbag, and quickdraws. Relative to big-wall aid climbing, this is a light-duty gear list. However, serious sport climbing wears out ropes, shoes, and harnesses quicker than other disciplines. So, with each item I've included a section on when to retire it. Always err on the side of safety. If you notice something about your gear that makes you question its integrity, replace it.

SHOES

Climbing shoes have the distinction of being the only piece of gear that can actually help you climb better.

Beginners are often told to buy "beginner" or "all-around" shoes—climbing footwear that's typically flat, stiff, and roomy in the toe box. Though "comfortable," these shoes provide about as much accuracy as one would need to shoot a basketball into a swimming pool.

No matter what your abilities are, consider getting a "high-precision" shoe—something that fits snugly and has a slight downturn to the toe—right off the bat. The benefit of wearing a high-performance shoe is that you will become more aware of how you place your toes on footholds. Beginner's shoes are often so stiff that they prevent learning the toe awareness needed to properly edge and toe down.

Also consider buying *three* different pairs of shoes, and bring two pairs to every crag. One pair should be down-turned, or "aggressive," for steep routes. The second pair should be flatter, making it more comfortable and supportive for warm-up routes or vertical faces. Pick up a cheap bouldering slipper for the third pair, and use it for your midweek gym/bouldering/training sessions. This triad of footwear prolongs shoe life and keeps toes from getting too worked or deformed by the repetitiveness of wearing one model for everything.

Velcro, laces, slippers. Laces are the most adjustable. Velcro is a compromise between fit and convenience; they are easy to get on and off. Slippers tend to be not as secure—if the slipper doesn't fit perfectly, it may slide off on heel hooks.

Stiffness. Go for "medium" stiffness. Too stiff, and the performance will be compromised; too soft, and your toes will pump out. A shoe's stiffness is relative to the person wearing it—a heavier person will need a stiffer model.

Last. The last is the shape of the shoe. Shoes come in straight, toe-down, and asymmetrical lasts, and depending on how your foot is shaped and what type of routes you want to climb, one of these lasts will work.

Lined/unlined. Some shoes have an in-

Fig. 3-1. A flat-lasted shoe with laces versus a more "aggressive" Velcro slipper with a slight downturn

ner lining, some don't. Lined shoes stretch less and have less sensitivity. Take this into account when choosing a size. Also, lined shoes tend to retain more odor.

A PERFECT FIT

Always try shoes on first—check out different models and different companies. Size them snugly: not too tight, but with no room to wiggle your toes. Avoid wearing socks with your climbing shoes because they decrease sensitivity and performance. How's the heel? Dead space in the heel is bad. If you can remove your foot from the heel while the laces are tied, try going down a half size. Stand around in the pair for at least five minutes—if you're in *serious* pain, go up a half size. Most shoes will break in. If you go up a half size and there's now too much room in the heel, switch to a different brand or model.

Women's fit. Many companies make models for women, and they are usually just a lower-volume version of another shoe in their line. If you have a narrow foot check out the women's line, even if you are a dude.

When to retire. When a hole appears in the rubber under the big toe, either buy a new pair or get your shoes resoled. Resoling may cost one-third of the original price tag, and a good cobbler can make your shoe like new. For odor, try sticking your shoes in the freezer for a few days. The cold kills much of the odor-causing bacteria.

HARNESS

A harness is a ticket to a wild place that few people on earth get to visit. It's also as intimate as underwear, and since you'll be spending a lot of time in it, you better find a harness that is comfortable, primarily on your lower back and legs.

A good sport harness is light and sleek, but also supportive. You'll be thankful for the support when you have to hold the weight of your hangdogging partner as he takes an hour to figure out the moves on a new project.

Harnesses come in an array of designs, all offering different features tailored to one type of climbing or another. It's best to find a harness you like and simply use it for everything, regardless of its advertised niche.

For sport climbing you will likely want a harness with as few buckles as possible (e.g. one with "fixed" leg loops, not the adjustable kind). Wearing a harness around a gear store doesn't really tell you much about how it will feel when you're hanging, falling, and belaying in it. In general, heavier climbers will want something with more padding, while lighter climbers won't need the extra bulk. Some harnesses integrate mesh, which breathes better and will be less sweaty in hot weather.

When to retire. Harnesses wear down at the lower tie-in point because the rope rubs and abrades this area every time you fall, hang, lower, or weight the rope. It's true that nylon sewn together keeps us safe, a crazy idea that works as long as we don't take it for granted. Get a new harness as soon as you see signs of wear, especially on the critical areas such as the belay loop and the tie-in points.

HARNESS PARTS AND OPERATION

Align the harness so the belay loop is facing front. Make sure there are no twists in the webbing connecting the leg loops. Step in through each leg loop and pull the harness up around your waist. You want the "swami belt" to sit at or just above your hip bones.

The most important thing to remember with your harness is that all of its buckles must be "doubled back," which means the webbing is threaded through the buckle once, then back through the first opening of the buckle.

Swami belt and buckle. Some harnesses

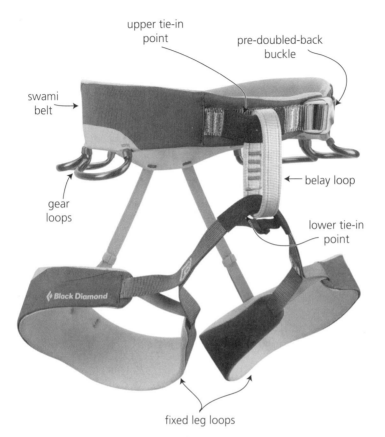

upper tie-in point

pre-doubled-back buckle

swami belt

belay loop

gear loops

lower tie-in point

fixed leg loops

Fig. 3-2. A good four–gear loop sport-climbing harness

come out of the package doubled-back, and all you have to do is cinch back the webbing to tighten the swami belt around your waist. Others require you to manually double back the webbing through the buckles. The former models adjust more quickly and virtually eliminate the danger of not doubling-back. Harnesses will come undone if they are not doubled back.

Tighten the harness so that it's snug, but not so tight that your breath is restricted.

Belay loop. A belay loop is a single loop of webbing—sometimes called "the donut"—that is stitched together with extremely strong bar-tacks. The belay loop connects the swami belt to the leg loops, and most belay loops hold 25 kilonewtons, or roughly 5600 pounds. This single stitch of webbing is the most important part of any harness. Belay loops are primarily used to clip your belay/rappel device to your harness via a locking carabiner. You will also be using your belay loop to clip you directly to anchors and bolts (see "Go In Direct," chapter 4). This is not only your lifeline if you are cleaning an anchor, but your partners depend on it to keep them safe, too. Inspect the entire belay loop regularly.

Tie-in points. The belay loop runs through the two tie-in points of a harness—the "lower" tie-in point is at the leg loops, while the upper one is at the swami belt. When you tie in to the rope, always thread the rope through the lower tie-in point first, then the upper one, and then complete your knot. Be sure to regularly inspect the lower tie-in point for wear. Also, *don't* clip your belay carabiner through the tie-in points, as some climbers do. Only clip the belay carabiner to the belay loop.

Gear loops. Gear loops are used for racking quickdraws and other gear such as belay devices. Gear loops are not meant to safely bear a climber's weight. Do not clip into an anchor via a gear loop. Some harnesses only come with two gear loops. Four gear loops are more versatile and add virtually no weight.

ROPES

A rope is the most expensive piece of gear you will purchase as a sport climber, typically costing between $150 and $300. It's also the most important piece of gear you'll own.

Fig. 3-3. (a) A healthy rope core has rigidity. (b) A damaged rope core is "flat," and can be pressed together.

For free climbing, the type of rope used is "dynamic," as opposed to "static." Dynamic ropes stretch when they are weighted; static ropes don't. Dynamic ropes *significantly* reduce the force a fall places on the gear, belayer, and climber. The amount a dynamic rope stretches in a fall depends on rope diameter, how much rope is out in the system, and differences in manufacturing.

How long? Just over a decade ago, the standard rope length was 50 meters (165 feet). Back then many sport routes reflected this standard by never being longer than 25 meters. These days, a 60-meter (200-foot) rope is standard and 30-meter routes are more common. It's now common for sport climbers to own 70- and 80-meter ropes.

The length of your rope will depend on how long the routes are at your home crag. If you climb at an area that's only 40 feet tall, you obviously don't need an 80-meter rope unless you plan on taking trips to southern France, where 80-meter ropes are needed. Another factor to consider is how much weight you want to carry. Longer ropes are obviously heavier.

However, consider this: sport climbing puts tremendous wear and tear on ropes. Falling can abrade the sheath at the fall point (about 5–7 feet in from your knot) in a matter of weeks, and sometimes in a single pitch. When this happens, you will have to cut the first 5–10 feet off the bad end, steadily hacking away at your rope.

Buying a longer rope makes sense. For $20–40 more, you can upgrade from a 60-meter rope to a 70-meter, giving 30 extra feet to trim before your rope becomes too short to use on 30-meter pitches. A longer rope also means you will be less likely to lower your partner off the end of the rope.

Many climbers are in the habit of marking the middle of their rope using a Sharpie. A middle mark can come in handy; however, as soon as you cut/trim your rope ends, the middle mark becomes erroneous.

The best bet is to keep a log of how long your rope is, and to know how long the routes are that you climb.

How thick? Dynamic single ropes come as thin as 8.9mm and as thick as 11mm. Chris Sharma says he doesn't climb on anything under 9.7mm thick. "I'm kind of a big guy," says the aw-shucks, six-foot-tall, 170-pound climber. Indeed, the heavier you are, the thicker the rope you will want. Of course, the thicker the rope is, the heavier it will be. On a long route, a thin rope creates *significantly* less rope drag. Just recently, 10mm and thicker ropes were standard. Now, few sport climbers go for anything with such girth—9.4–9.8mm is standard. Anything thinner starts feeling pretty skimpy.

If you get a 70- or 80-meter rope but are worried about weight, compensate with a thinner diameter. A 70-meter 9.1mm Maxim Apogee weighs 8.5 pounds, over a full pound less than a 70-meter 9.9mm Maxim Apex (9.8 pounds).

Dry or non-dry? Some ropes come standard with a "dry treatment," while others require paying more for the coating that repels water and ice. A dry coating is definitely worth it, though, providing extra protection and life.

When to retire? Inspect your cord every time you climb. A little fuzz on the sheath is normal and nothing to be worried about. A rope's main strength is in its core, not the sheath. When you pinch a small bight of rope together, there should be enough rigidity to the core to create a small gap (figure 3-3). If you can pinch a small bight completely together so it's touching itself, you have a "soft spot," which means the core is weakened and potentially damaged. If this soft spot is near the rope end, it's no big deal: just trim the cord above the damaged area. If you find a soft spot in the middle of the rope, retire the rope.

Throw away any rope that comes into contact with sulfuric or battery acid. In one frightening incident, a rope that had been merely placed on a driveway with spilt battery acid later *cut in half* when a leader took a modest fall in an indoor gym (the climber was okay). Even the vapors of a car battery have been shown to compromise nylon's integrity. Store your rope in a rope bag and away from strong acids.

Instead of throwing your rope out, please recycle your cord with Sterling's Rope Recycling Initiative. See www.sterlingrope.com/recycling.

HOW TO TRIM YOUR ROPE

Have your partner hold the rope taut while you apply, as tightly as possible, two or three wraps of athletic tape right above the part you want to cut.

With a knife, saw the rope right next to the tape. The tighter your partner keeps the line, the cleaner the cut will be.

Use a lighter to melt the cut nylon so it doesn't unravel. Singe it until it's black.

ROPE BAG

A rope bag keeps your cord out of the dirt, clean and protected from UV light or chemicals. A rope bag also keeps your rope flaked, making it easier to migrate to the next route. Rope bags usually have a loop for tying rope ends—a feature originally designed to organize the top and bottom ends of a flaked rope. Tie the bottom end of the rope to the tarp's loop with a big knot, and you'll never lower your partner off the end of your rope.

QUICKDRAWS

Quickdraws have three parts to them: the top biner that gets clipped to a bolt hanger, the bottom biner that gets clipped to the rope, and the "dogbone," or webbing, that connects the two.

Some quickdraws use wire-gate biners, some use straight- or bent-gate biners, and some have a combination of both. Wire gates are lighter and are less likely to come unclipped, making them perfect for the rope-end of the draw.

Use quickdraws that have two distinctly different biners (e.g., all top biners are red with straight gates, while all bottom biners are green with wire gates). The top biner is just for clipping bolts, while the bottom biner is just for clipping the rope. Do not mix up the two! Bolt hangers dig sharp, notched grooves into the soft aluminum of the top carabiner after catching repeated falls, and you don't want your rope running over that.

The most important part of a quickdraw is the dogbone. Buy draws with bones that are thick, durable, and made of nylon. The lightweight 10mm Spectra dogbones may reduce overall weight, but they are

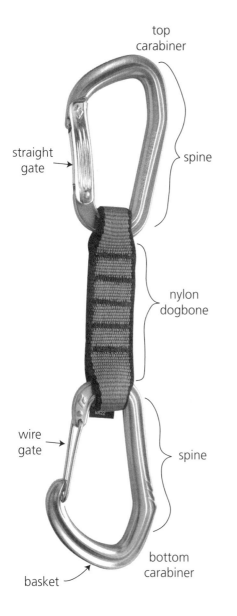

top
carabiner

straight
gate

spine

nylon
dogbone

wire
gate

spine

basket

bottom
carabiner

Fig. 3-4. A good sport-climbing quickdraw

significantly more difficult to grab. Further, these thin Spectra bones don't withstand the wear and tear of hanging on a route for an extended period of time as well as nylon bones do. A good quickdraw will also have a rubber piece in the dogbone to keep the bottom carabiner from spinning. The top carabiner of a quickdraw has more wiggle room, which is a safety feature when the rope shifts quickdraws around on bolts— and is yet another reason not to confuse the top carabiner with the bottom one.

A rack of 12 draws is an average minimum. Eventually you'll want 30 or more: enough to leave half hanging on a long-term project, while using the other half for warm-up routes or climbing elsewhere. Many climbers are uncomfortable with the idea of leaving their gear hanging on a route, but in most areas leaving quickdraws on a route for a week or two is standard. Other climbers will climb on your quickdraws, just as at some point you will climb on theirs.

Nevertheless, if you are climbing in an access-sensitive area, it's best not to leave your draws up. Also, if you see quickdraws hanging on a route, you should not take them! They aren't yours, and stealing climbing gear is bad karma.

When to retire. Routinely inspect both carabiners. A little notch in a quickdraw's top carabiner won't cause failure. Use more prudence with the rope-end carabiner, which will develop deep, sharp grooves from the rope running over it. A deep groove weakens the biner, while a sharp groove could cut your rope.

When clipping draws that someone else has left hanging on a route, always inspect every biner you clip. Also inspect the dogbone. Look for abrasions or cuts in the nylon, and replace anything that looks worn. Retire nylon that is faded from UV rays—the compromise in strength is slight, but not worth keeping around.

BELAY DEVICES

Belay devices fall into two categories: autolocking and passive/standard. For sport climbing, an autolocking belay device is the way to go. (See chapter 8 for belay-device usage.)

Passive devices are the classic belay plates such as the ATC. They are cheap (under $20) and light, and, unlike autolocking devices, ATCs can be used to rappel down two ropes. Belay plates vary in design and style, but they all basically function the same way. Some devices such as the Black Diamond ATC Guide and the Petzl Reverso can be used in an autolocking mode when belaying a second from above.

But for single-pitch sport climbing, an autolocking device is highly recommended. Autolocking devices provide additional security in sport climbing, where unexpected falls occur frequently. They also hold a hangdogging partner's weight effortlessly. There are a handful of autolocking devices on the market, but the one that has withstood the test of time is the Petzl Grigri.

When to retire. After years of use, all belay devices get worn from the friction of

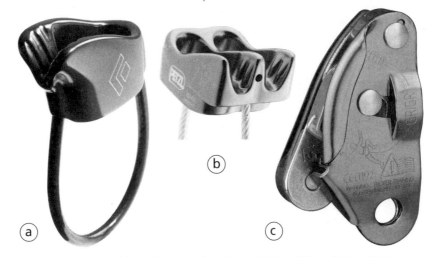

Fig. 3-5. Three belay devices: (a) Black Diamond ATC-Sport (b) Petzl Verso (c) Petzl Grigri

Fig. 3-6. Two specialty belay carabiners: (a) Petzl Freino (b) DMM Belay Master

a rope running over their edges. A visual inspection of the wear confirms whether or not the device needs replacing. The internal cam of a Grigri will wear down, over time making the device less secure with thinner ropes. (See chapter 8.)

BELAY-DEVICE CARABINERS

A large pear-shaped locking carabiner pairs best with an ATC. Any locking biner will work with a Grigri, but consider these two special ones.

The DMM Belay Master is a pear-shaped locking carabiner outfitted with a plastic plate between its two axes. The plastic piece folds over and locks onto the gate, which keeps the carabiner from "crossloading," which is a potentially dangerous situation in which a Grigri shifts from the carabiner basket to the carabiner spine and is then loaded

COLLECT LEAVER BINERS

Keep carabiners that are older but not worn to use as "leaver biners." It's a good idea to keep one on your harness at all times. If you need to bail off a route, simply clip your leaver biner to a bolt and lower. (However, keep in mind that lowering off only one carabiner is never the safest choice.) Also use a leaver biner to replace a bad biner on a fixed draw, even (especially) if it's not yours. A leaver biner may also come in handy at an anchor, where fixed carabiners tend to be most worn.

when the climber falls. Carabiners are designed to be loaded at only two points: the two curved ends of the carabiner. The straight parts of the carabiner—the gate and, parallel to it, the spine—are not meant to be loaded. When a carabiner is loaded on the sides, it is called cross-loading, and it's very dangerous because the carabiner is four times weaker in a sideways position. The DMM Belay Master prevents cross-loading. The Petzl Freino is a unique autolocking carabiner that has an integrated wire-gate spur on the outside of the main axis. When lowering a climber, you have the option to run the rope against this spur, which creates additional friction and makes lowering your partner easier. This extra control is especially handy when using ropes of smaller diameters or lowering heavier climbers.

BELAY GLOVES

Pick up a pair of leather gloves from a gardening or hardware store, or throw down for the burlier ones made by many climbing companies. More than anything, belay gloves keep your hands grease- and grime-free—important for maintaining high skin friction. Belay gloves also provide more control than bare hands when lowering a partner.

HELMET

Helmets have never been lighter and more comfortable, and there's no excuse not to wear one, especially as you learn the art of falling. Also, just because you see bolts and chalk doesn't guarantee that a chunk

LEAVE THE DAISY CHAINS AT HOME!

Daisy chains are nylon or Spectra tethers with many loops sewn into them that some climbers affix to their belay loops to clip into anchors or bolts. However, daisy chains are not recommended for sport climbing.

Leaving a daisy chain permanently fixed to your belay loop is a potentially dangerous idea. First, daisy chains get in the way. They also tend to become a permanent fixture on many harnesses. A daisy chain that has been girth-hitched to the same point on the belay loop for an extended period of time welds itself on there, potentially obstructing your view of any damage to the belay loop. Fixed daisy chains also focus the wear and tear on single points on the belay loop. Many have speculated that the tragedy of sport-climbing pioneer Todd Skinner's broken belay loop was due to the sawing action created by his fixed daisy chains.

Instead of using a daisy chain, use a "dogging draw"—just a regular quickdraw you always keep on your harness—to clip directly to bolts while working your project. Clipping directly to a bolt while on route is called "going in direct."

of rock won't come down and clock you. Climbing areas are still wild places, and it's always a good idea to wear a helmet, even when you're belaying. The best and safest helmets are the lightweight foam models as opposed to the Kevlar-shell ones.

CHALKBAG AND CHALK

Find a chalkbag that is cool and fits your whole hand. Some are shallower than others, and some are wider.

Don't clip your chalkbag to your harness with a carabiner since it renders the bag askew. Using a piece of webbing, nylon string, or even a lightweight belt, tie the chalkbag around your waist. To keep the chalkbag from riding up your torso, try threading the strand through the belay loop. A chalkbag should have a brush holder, too—one that accommodates a wide range of brush sizes.

There are different brands of loose chalk on the market, in addition to premade chalk balls. You need to squeeze chalk balls to get the chalk out of them, which is more tiring. Chalk balls also tend to fall out when a climber is hanging upside down. The loose stuff is messier but applies quicker.

Get a chalk bucket—basically an oversized chalkbag—and use it to store a greater stash of loose chalk. Bring your chalk bucket with you to the crags and draw from it to replenish your chalkbag.

Liquid chalk—essentially a blend of alcohol and chalk—is excellent when the humidity is up or the beginning of the route is bouldery and difficult. Applying a little dollop of liquid chalk to your hands right before you climb allows you to climb longer and farther without having to apply the loose stuff. To apply liquid chalk, place a dime-sized dollop in each hand and rub it in, especially working it over the fingertips. Let the alcohol dry by waving your hands through the air. A white, ultradry residue is left in place—this is a good base layer for adding yet another layer of regular loose chalk.

Liquid chalk really dries out your skin and can cause it to crack and break so use liquid chalk sparingly. Make sure you moisturize your hands at the end of any climbing day, especially if you've been using liquid chalk.

BRUSHES

Get a brush and keep it with your chalkbag. A stiff nylon brush is light and functional. Boar's hair brushes are softer and don't work as well on really grimy/dirty/muddy rock. However, nothing takes chalk off slopers and crimpers better than a boar's hair brush. Toothbrushes are okay (try a denture toothbrush) but wear down quicker. Don't use wire brushes! They erode rock, especially sandstone. It's good style to scrub a few holds when lowering down a route.

KNEEPADS

Just as sticky rubber shoes and chalk were once considered "cheating" by some climbers because they made routes significantly easier, so now are kneepads and kneebarring. This technique—essentially no different than hand jamming or stemming—has dropped entire number grades off cruxes. Of course some routes will be harder if you don't know how to hand jam; similarly some routes will be harder if you don't know how to kneebar.

Climbers now employ kneepads with rubber, not only to increase friction between leg and stone, but also to alleviate the pain of mashing their thighs into a sharp fin of rock.

HOW TO MAKE KNEEPADS

Go to a sports store (or pharmacy) and get two "closed-knee" neoprene support sleeves. You don't want the kind with a hole in it, but the closed kind such as those made by McDavid.

Though these neoprene sleeves are meant to be worn *over* injured knees, you will actually pull the kneepad all the way up above the patella and around the bare

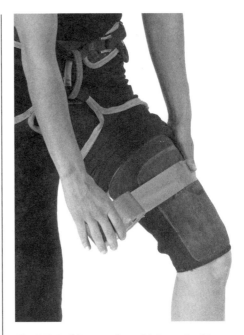

Fig. 3-7. Pull kneepad up thigh, and add a wrap of duct tape (optional) to keep it from sliding.

KEEP THAT KNEEPAD ON!

For most situations on most routes, a tight, well-fitting kneepad won't slide around or off. However, some kneebars are so demanding that your pad will slide out of place. Here are two common fixes:

Use duct tape. Two snug (not tight) wraps of duct tape around the kneepad at the top of the pad/thigh are often sufficient. Some climbers tape the pad right to thigh skin.

Use spray tape. Pre-tape tape adherent, sold at most sports stores, can be used to temporarily glue the kneepad to your skin. After putting the pad on, roll up the pad at the bottom (at the kneecap) so that the inside is showing. Spray some pre-tape onto the inside of the pad and the top of your knee, and let it dry before rolling your pads back down. Pre-tape leaves a sticky residue on your skin but it works like a charm. (Also, use pre-tape as a base when taping up an injured finger with athletic tape, otherwise the tape will come off midroute.)

skin of your thigh. (Ideally you'll be wearing shorts, but you can also size the kneepads larger and wear them over pants). Try a pad on in the store. Pull it up so that the bottom of the pad is just above the kneecap. You want the smallest size you can squeeze into.

Get a 4x8-inch sheet of climbing-shoe rubber from a climbing-shoe resoler or directly from the manufacturer. If you need to, cut the rectangular sheet so that it fits on the neoprene sleeve, covering most of the top thigh. Focus on how wide the rubber is right above the kneecap. You want the rubber to be just wider than your kneecap. The rubber also needs to be flush with the bottom of the pad. However, it doesn't need to go all the way up to the top of the pad—cut it so it goes an inch or two shy of the top.

Have a cobbler glue or sew the climbing shoe rubber to the neoprene sleeve. Make sure the cobbler places the rubber on correctly: right to the very bottom edge of the pad.

Some shoe resolers, such as Rock and Resole in Boulder, Colorado, are now selling premade kneepads.

STICK CLIP

Stick clips are telescopic painters' poles with devices at one end that allow you to clip the rope into a quickdraw, or a quickdraw to a bolt that is out of reach. Climbers use stick clips to create temporary top ropes, and on some routes stick clipping the first bolt is a good idea for safety reasons. Remember, sport climbing is about minimizing risk in order to focus on the difficulty of the movement. There's no reason to risk a ground fall. Sometimes, for the sake of minimizing fixed gear, route equippers establish routes with the intention of people stick clipping the first bolt.

To make a stick clip, buy an extendable painter's pole with screw threads from a hardware store. The Rock Climbing Tools Superclip simply screws right on and is

JOIN THE REVOLUTION

The DMM Revolver is a unique carabiner that has one great application to sport climbing. Equipped with a pulley built into the carabiner's basket, the Revolver reduces rope drag and friction. Because the first quickdraw of a sport route often endures the most friction, using a Revolver for the rope-end carabiner of the first quickdraw makes boinking, winching, and falling much smoother for both the belayer and climber.

ready to go. This device not only allows you to clip draws to bolts and ropes to draws, but also to actually remove draws that are hanging on bolts.

Another option is to make your own. To do so, pick up a rubberized bench spring clamp and two hose clamps while you're at the hardware store. Affix one leg of the spring clamp to the top of the extendable stick with the two hose clamps. (See chapter 7 for more on stick clipping.)

USEFUL MISCELLANEOUS ITEMS

Nail clippers, duct tape (for kneepads), athletic tape (for taping up torn finger skin), lighter and knife (for trimming a rope), vitamin E oil (for restoring fingertip skin), Neosporin (the pain-killing kind), lip balm, small tube of moisturizing cream (for post-climbing skin hydration), emergency headlamp, energy gel.

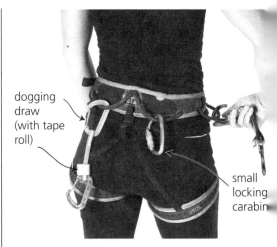

dogging draw (with tape roll)

small locking carabiner

Fig. 3-8. Outfit your harness with these items.

CLOTHING

Wear appropriate layers. Bring a pair of shorts with you in case you want to use kneepads. Buy a warm puffie and make sure it has two large mesh pouches on the inside. Put your shoes in these pouches to

HOT ROCKS

Completely numb fingers can be one of the most frustrating, and *gripping,* problems a climber will face on cold days. It is quite unsettling when you can't feel whether you're grabbing a hold or not. One solution is the instant hand-warmers sold at most sport stores; keep one of the packets in your chalkbag if cold hands are a concern. An even better option is to bring a small camping stove to the crag. Heat up a a few small rocks by placing them directly into the stove's flame for about a minute. Put the warm rocks in your chalkbag right before you climb. Stones heated over a flame emit much more warmth than hand-warmer packets. Espresso or tea is also a pleasant treat on a cold day.

SETTING UP YOUR RIG

keep the rubber warm in between burns. Cold (45 degrees or below) rubber is less sticky. A good pair of sport-climbing pants will be durable and won't tear easily, but will be loose enough to allow you to easily move into splits, stems, and high steps.

SETTING UP YOUR RIG

Style out your harness by keeping these items with you at all times. The ropework techniques described in this book require you to have a dogging draw and a small locking carabiner.

Dogging draw. Keep one ultralightweight quickdraw on your harness. You'll need it when working routes, but it can also be used as a backup if a draw is missing on a route. Some climbers also keep a small roll of athletic tape on their harness by threading the quickdraw's dogbone through the tape roll.

Small locking carabiner. You'll use this when threading anchors to lower, or when pulling the rope and retying in midroute. (See chapters 4 and 8.)

Leaver biner. Keep a leaver biner with you, preferably a locking biner. Another option is a medium-sized steel quicklink, which costs only $3 at hardware stores and is cheaper than leaving a carabiner if you need to bail midroute.

CHAPTER 4

The author top-roping on a 5.12a at Shelf Road, Colorado (Photo © Keith Ladzinski)

Starting Out: Tying In, Top-roping, and Cleaning an Anchor

Getting up and down a sport route safely is relatively simple compared to other forms of roped climbing. This is a mixed blessing: it opens the joy of climbing to anyone with a harness, rope, and belayer; but it also sometimes invites a careless attitude, as evinced by the number of easily preventable accidents that occur at sport crags across the country every year. Sport climbing accidents happen to both beginners and experts alike. In the 1990s Lynn Hill was in the middle of tying her knot when she stopped to put on a coat. Preoccupied, she forgot to finish tying her knot, and her partners didn't check carefully enough. She climbed to the chains, said "Take," and fell 70 feet to the ground, miraculously sustaining only minor injuries. Many accidents like this occur because we get lazy or become inured by the repetitiveness of the act. Though the primary focus of sport climbing is to enjoy and improve one's free climbing, it's paramount to master the basic technical skills and to always stay focused on safety.

Sport climbing can be truly safe—but only if we are committed to making it so.

HOW SPORT CLIMBING WORKS

It takes two to tango. A leader ties into one end of a rope, typically 200 feet long. A belayer attaches the rope to his harness using a locking carabiner and belay device.

The leader/belayer dyad is the most fundamental and sacred relationship in all of climbing, involving mutual trust, respect, and skill.

After checking to make sure the harnesses, belay device, and rope are safely loaded, the leader starts moving up a rock face that has bolts drilled into the wall, usually anywhere from 4 to 12 feet apart (and longer in some areas, especially in parts of Europe). If a route has eight bolts, the leader brings up ten quickdraws in order to clip into each of the eight bolts, plus the two bolts at the end of the route that compose the anchor. As the leader progresses upward, the belayer feeds out rope through the belay device, staying with the climber as he progresses up the wall.

When the leader reaches a bolt, he removes one quickdraw from his harness and clips it to the bolt's steel hanger. He pulls up just enough rope to clip into the bottom carabiner of the quickdraw. He then continues climbing.

If the leader falls, the belayer holds the rope and the belay device locks down, preventing any more rope from coming out. The leader will fall until the rope comes taut on the most recently clipped quickdraw. If a leader is 4 feet *above* a quickdraw, he will take at least an 8-foot fall, plus rope stretch.

When the leader reaches the anchor, he clips the rope to the anchor bolts using two more quickdraws. The leader yells "Take!" to the belayer. The belayer *takes in* the remaining slack until he feels the leader's weight. When the leader calls down to be lowered, the belayer lowers him through the belay device on the second half of the rope. Thus, if a route is 100 feet long, a 200-foot rope is needed to lower from the anchors.

FIVE VITAL CHECKS BEFORE ANYONE CLIMBS
1) Climber's knot is properly tied.
2) Climber's harness is doubled back.
3) Belayer's harness is doubled back.
4) Belay device is properly loaded.
5) Belay carabiner is locked.

Check and double-check these five things before anyone leaves the ground. Always employ a dialogue of questions to address each of these checks, like so:

Belayer: "Are your knot and harness good?" (Both inspect climber's knot and harness.)

Climber: "Yes, my knot's good, and I am doubled back. Am I on belay?" (Both inspect belay device, belay carabiner, and belayer's harness.)

Belayer: "Yes, you're on belay. Climb when ready."

Climber: "Shig-a-dang, I'm climbing!"

When the lead climber reaches the ground, the belayer, who is on deck to top-rope, will tie in to the other end of the rope—the side that is clipped through all of the quickdraws. The leader pulls his end of the rope through the anchor until it comes taut on the top roper. Now it's the lead climber's turn to be the belayer.

The top roper climbs up and removes each quickdraw until he reaches the anchors. The top roper does NOT simply unclip the rope from quickdraws at the anchor, but rather he goes "in direct" (uses two quickdraws to clip his harness to the anchor) and then "cleans" it. This chapter explains how to get started with ropes and gear, how to top-rope, and how to clean an anchor.

complex. You must remember to tie your knot, double-back your harness, load the belay device, clip carabiners properly, and communicate with your belayer, often in fast succession and under stress. The simpler you can make things, the better. In sport climbing the variables almost never change: there's a route with some number of bolts and an anchor at its end. It's amazing how creative some climbers can get with something as simple as lowering down a sport climb. What's not amazing is how often these divergences from the proven, simple path result in accidents. Make sure you and your belayer are always on the same page. Keep things simple and keep it safe.

KISS

Before going any further, it's worth stressing a seldom-vocalized principle that needs to be ingrained in every climber: Keep It Simple, Stupid! Rock climbing is

THE PERFECT KNOT: HOW TO TIE IN

Tying your knot correctly is the most important safety issue in all of climbing. Climbers use one of these two knots to tie

FOUR RULES FOR TYING ONE ON
1) When threading the rope through the harness, always go through the lower tie-in point first, then through the upper tie-in point on the swami belt.
2) Tie your knot as close to your harness as possible. This prevents the potentially awkward situation of your knot getting stuck in a carabiner while climbing.
3) Always "dress" your knot, meaning there are no kinks or twists.
4) No tie-in knot is complete until you tie a backup knot. While the backup knot doesn't add any strength to the main knot, it ensures that there's enough tail so that the main knot will not come undone.

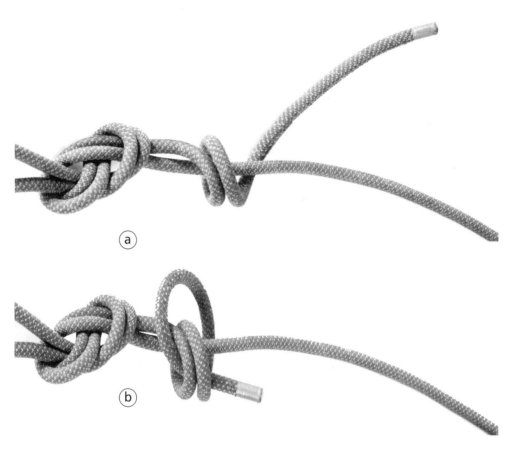

Fig. 4-1. Stopper knot

in to the end of a rope: the retraced figure eight, and the double bowline. Pick the one you prefer and stick with it.

STOPPER KNOT

A stopper knot is the backup knot traditionally used to complete the figure eight and double bowline.

- Take the tail and wrap it around the main rope twice right next to the tie-in knot (figure 4-1a). You want your stopper knot close to the tie-in knot.
- Bring the tail down and then back up through the loops you just created (figure 4-1b).
- Pull it tight; cinch it down.

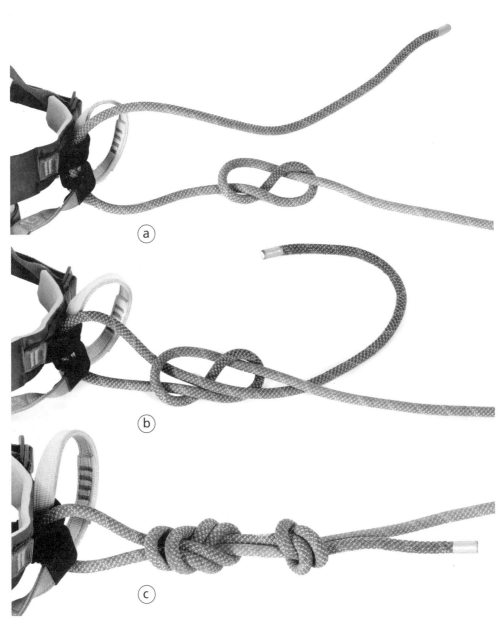

Fig. 4-2. Retraced figure eight

RETRACED FIGURE EIGHT

The figure eight is simple to tie, easy to inspect, and the tried-and-true knot preferred by most climbers.

- Take about an arm's length of rope from the end.
- Tie an "8" into the rope by twisting the rope one and a half times and threading the end through the top twist.
- Thread the end through both tie-in points on your harness, lower tie-in point first. (See figure 4-2a.)
- Pull the rope until the figure eight is close to your harness. Retrace the end *back through* the figure eight exactly. After completely retracing the knot, there should be a minimum of 6–8 inches of "tail" leftover. (See figure 4-2b.)
- Use the excess tail to tie a stopper knot. (See figure 4-2c.)

Alternate finish: The "sport tuck" involves simply tucking the tail back into the knot. (See figure 4-3.) The advantage with this finish is the knot is less bulky and perhaps makes the figure eight a bit easier to untie. It doesn't compromise the knot's strength.

To untie a figure eight that's been loaded in a fall, push the main end of the rope into the knot. Now "break it" by grabbing either side of the 8 and bending the knot like a twig you want to snap until it works loose.

Fig. 4-3. Retraced figure eight, alternate finish

DOUBLE BOWLINE

Though harder to learn than the figure eight, the double bowline becomes quicker (and therefore easier) to tie once you've got it down. Plus, the double bowline is sleeker, less likely to get caught in a quickdraw, and much easier to untie, especially after being loaded by a fall, than a figure eight.

◼ Take the rope end and thread it through the harness tie-in points, bottom one first. Pull up about a foot of rope.

◼ Now take the main side of the rope and make a double loop by wrapping it around your pointer finger. Your finger should be pointed up toward you, and the loops should spiral up, too. (See figure 4-4a.)

◼ Take the tail and thread it down through the two loops. (See figure 4-4b.)

◼ Weave the tail over the front side of the main rope. Thread it through the double loops so it comes out the same side it went in. (See figure 4-4c.)

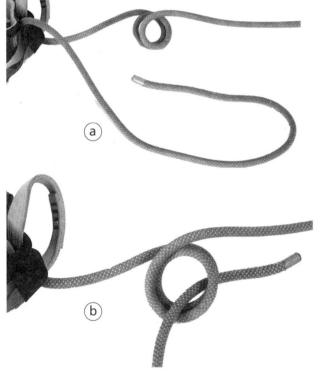

Fig. 4-4. Double bowline

Cinch the knot by pulling on the tail and the main rope at the same time, so that it's properly dressed and compact. Tie a stopper knot in between the double bowline and the upper tie-in point on the harness. (See figure 4-4d.) Notice that this stopper knot is upside-down compared to the stopper knot used in the figure eight. Tuck excess tail back through the upper tie-in point.

FIGURE EIGHT ON A BIGHT

If you can tie a retraced figure eight to your harness, this knot is a cinch. It's a great knot for clipping into the middle of the rope when threading/cleaning an anchor or when pulling the rope through midroute (see chapter 7).

- Start with an 8-inch bight of rope.
- Tie a figure eight into the line using both strands of the bight (figure 4-5a).
- Dress the knot and cinch it down (figure 4-5b).

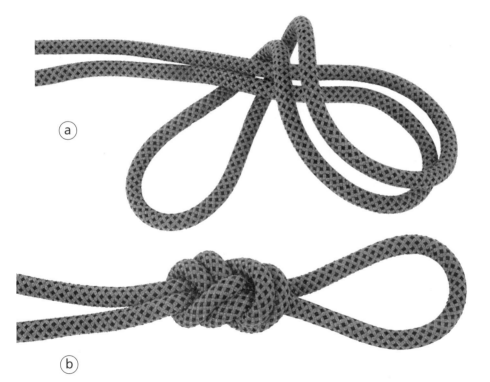

Fig. 4-5. Figure eight on a bight

HOW TO TOP-ROPE

Beginners are usually introduced to rock climbing under the tutelage of a hired certified rock instructor or experienced friends. Either way, most beginners start out climbing with the safety of a rope pre-strung through overhead anchors: top-roping. If you're new to the sport, top-roping is a great way to become familiar and comfortable with the unusual and extraordinary experience of hanging from your fingers 60 feet off the ground. Top-roping strips away the risks of lead climbing and allows one to focus on learning how to move up and over rock.

While top-roping, you want to climb on the side of the rope clipped through the quickdraws because if you fall the quickdraws prevent you from swinging away from the wall. When you reach a quickdraw, you have to unclip it from the rope. As with leading, you want to find a good stance from which to unclip a quickdraw before moving up. Typically it's easiest to unclip when the quickdraw is at your chest or waist—not above your head.

To easily unclip the rope from a quickdraw, grab the rope just below the carabiner. Bring it around so that it's on the outside of the carabiner's gate. Place your middle finger in the carabiner basket to steady the quickdraw. Now simply press the rope through the gate. Alternately, hold the carabiner with your fingers, open the gate with your thumb, and slide the rope out of the carabiner by flicking your wrist. Forgetting to unclip a quickdraw is a common and unfortunate error that results in something called "top-rope surprise," which is the awkward moment you realize you can't move up any further because the still-clipped draw below your waist is pulling you back down and off the wall. Surprise! Try to downclimb a move and unclip the draw.

Falling while on top rope is a matter of simply letting go. You will drop about 1–3 feet due to stretch in the rope. The amount the rope stretches depends on the diameter of your rope (thinner ropes tend to stretch more), how much rope is "out" (the length of rope between you and the belayer; more rope out means more stretch), how much friction there is (a top rope clipped through ten quickdraws will stretch less than a rope not clipped through any quickdraws), and of course how heavy the climber is. Thus, if you're a heavy climber top-roping a long route that has hard moves at the start, be careful. Falling down low *could* mean that you will land on the ground. A great belayer (of equal weight) can help prevent some stretch, but there's only so much one can do.

When you fall on top rope, don't grab quickdraws, and never, ever grab a bolt hanger! Just let your body come away from the rock gently. This is intimidating at first. The more you do it the more you will learn that the gear actually works. Falling on top rope and gaining trust in the system is an important precursor to learning how to fall on lead.

When you arrive at the top of the climb, there's one primary thing to remember: **Don't unclip from the anchors!**

GETTING LOWERED

If you don't have to clean the anchor, or you don't know how, you will simply call down to your belayer to "Take!" and prepare to be lowered.

The belayer takes in all the remaining slack, and you will feel the rope come taut on your harness. Sit back and place your feet flat against the wall. As your belayer lowers you, use your feet to walk yourself down the wall, pushing off and maneuvering around any protrusions or roofs.

If there is another person in line to top-rope the same climb, you will want to clip your end of the rope back through the quickdraws as you lower past them. On slabby routes (anything under 90 degrees vertical), it's usually pretty easy to grab the quickdraws to do this. The key is to grab the quickdraw by the dogbone and pull yourself into it. Communicate with your belayer—tell him to "Hold on!" or "Lower just a bit more, please!" in order to get your rope back into the draw's biner.

On slightly overhanging routes it's more difficult to reach in and grab the quickdraws to clip back in as you are lowered. In fact it sometimes requires a dynamic bit of athleticism. One good trick is to use your legs to continually push off the wall as you are being lowered. Creating this swinging motion makes it possible to reach in at the perfect moment and snag the quickdraw. When trying to get into the wall, never try to push off the wall *toward* where you want to go; instead push out in the opposite direction of where you want

to go so that on the swing in, you swing right toward the draw or hold you are trying to reach.

TYPES OF ANCHORS

All good sport-climbing anchors are the same in that they are made up of two bolts with some kind of *smooth* metal surface—rings, chains, quicklinks, or carabiners—for lowering off.

Fixed carabiners. Most popular sport routes are equipped with fixed carabiners that make cleaning a route easier because you don't have to go in direct, untie, and clean the anchor—you simply clip the carabiners and lower. If the carabiners are standard aluminum ones, be wary. Aluminum carabiners wear down quickly and need to be replaced often. Inspect any fixed anchor carabiners for sharp grooves worn into the metal—feel it with your hand and look at the carabiner's basket. If you reach an anchor with bad biners, replace them with two of your own.

Steel carabiners are much more durable, but check them just the same. Fixed anchor carabiners are used to make lowering and cleaning draws easier. Don't top-rope through fixed anchor carabiners! Clip two of your own quickdraws directly to the bolt hangers and run the rope through them—when it's time to retrieve your gear, first clip the rope through the two fixed carabiners, then unclip your own quickdraws.

If the carabiners are clipped directly to the bolt hangers, be conscious of how you clip the rope in. Orient the biners so they are perpendicular to the rock and parallel to each other. When carabiners are clipped in such a way that one is twisted in relation to the other one, it kinks the rope *really* badly when you lower through it.

Rings. Fixe, a bolt and anchor company, sells standard bolt hangers with welded rings attached to them (figure 4-6a). You may see two individual bolts with rings side by side, or you may see a single ring

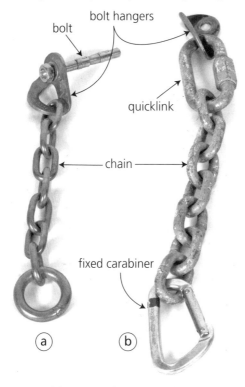

bolt hangers
bolt
quicklink
chain
fixed carabiner
(a)   (b)

Fig. 4-6. (a) Fixe ring/chain anchor (b) A chain clipped to bolt hanger via a quicklink with a fixed carabiner

attached to two bolts via a chain. Though there's only one ring in this latter setup, the anchor is still strong and redundant. Both these anchors will need to be cleaned.

Quicklinks/chains. Quicklinks attach chains to bolt hangers to create an anchor that's equalized, durable, and easy to lower off (figure 4-6b). Some older routes have smaller quicklinks that make running the rope through them difficult—if that's the case, you may need to simply leave two carabiners clipped to the chain.

Open cold-shuts. These steel hooks with wire-gate openings (figure 4-7) at the top are popular at some areas because they make clipping the anchor really easy. Simply drop the rope through the top wire gate into the basket. These anchors make it impossible to top-rope off of your own gear, so it's okay to top-rope through the cold-shuts. Since they are steel it will take years for them to wear down, at which point it will be the duty of an active member of the community to replace them.

Metolius rap hanger/welded cold-shuts. Metolius took the standard bolt hanger design and beefed it up to create a wide, smooth surface. Some older anchors use welded cold-shuts for the bolt hanger. These rounded smooth surfaces are okay to lower off, but not ideal since they make going in direct and threading the anchor more difficult.

Webbing. Rarely, you'll find anchors that are composed of two bolts with webbing threaded through them and equalized in a "V." There should be a rap ring or some kind of metal in place as well for lowering

Fig. 4-7. Fixe anchor hardware, with an open cold-shut shown front and center

off. *Note: Never run the rope directly over any webbing! Always remember: rope to metal only!* Webbing is bomber if you place it and tie it yourself, but the stuff that's been sitting out in the sun may be dangerous. If suspicious, clip your own carabiners directly to the bolt hangers and lower off of them. Webbing anchors at sport climbing areas should be replaced with chains.

HOW TO GO IN DIRECT

Going in direct means you use a quick-draw to clip yourself directly into a bolt or anchor so that your entire weight is on the fixed gear, not the rope. Going in direct has several applications in sport climbing, and you'll do it when you're leading, top-roping, cleaning an anchor, or cleaning the draws off a route.

Going in direct gives your belayer a break from holding your weight. Do it midroute when you need a rest. When leading, going in direct to a single bolt will also help you reach up to a higher bolt to preplace a quickdraw or clip the rope up to a higher bolt. (See chapter 7.)

Going in direct to one bolt does not mean you are off belay! Don't untie your knot, and don't let your belayer unclip you from the belay device. *You must be clipped to two separate bolts via two separate quickdraws to be both in direct and off belay.*

Fig. 4-8. "Going in direct" is a way to clip yourself to a bolt. Clip one end of your dogging draw to your belay loop and the other end to the bolt or quick draw. Going in direct has many applications in sport climbing.

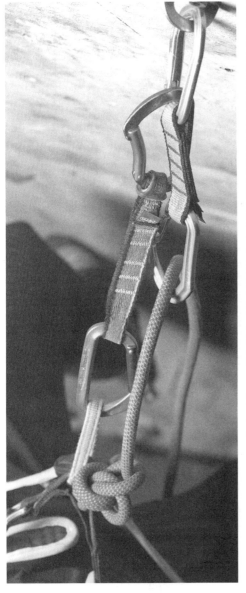

Fig. 4-9. Climber is now clipped in direct.

Here's how to go in direct to a single bolt with a quickdraw:

1) Take your dogging draw and clip it to your belay loop.
2) Grab the quickdraw hanging on the bolt, set your feet on the rock and pull/thrust your waist up toward this draw. (See figure 4-8.)
3) With your other hand, take your dogging draw and clip its top carabiner to the top carabiner of the route draw.
4) Let your weight settle onto the bolt (figure 4-9), and call down to your belayer, "I'm in direct."

CLEANING AN ANCHOR

Regardless of what type of anchors there are, cleaning them will involve the same basic steps. Cleaning an anchor means going in direct to the anchor's two points, untying your knot, and threading the rope through the rings, quicklinks, or cold-shuts. Next, you retie your knot and go back on belay; that means your belayer holds your weight on the fixed anchor gear, allowing you to retrieve your own gear. Knowing how to clean anchors will make you a much better partner, even if you haven't started leading climbs yet. Learning to clean an anchor must be practiced on the ground first. Ask your local gym to set up an anchor at the base of the indoor wall so you can practice.

Also called "threading the anchor," this crucial step is the most dangerous part of sport climbing. Most errors and tragedies are a result of poor communication

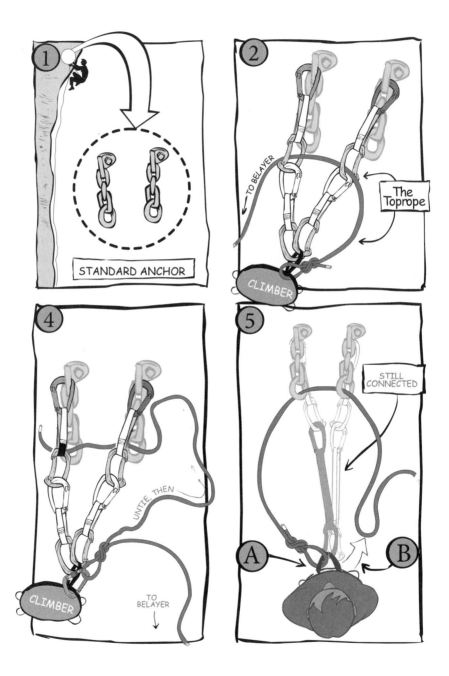

Fig. 4-10. Cleaning an anchor

between the climber at the anchor and the belayer on the ground.

Some climbers with trad backgrounds are unaccustomed to being lowered off a route, since they usually rappel from anchors. Cleaning draws on rappel is difficult, and often impossible if the route traverses or is steep. Get accustomed to being lowered off every sport route you climb.

Clipping in direct to an anchor. Upon reaching the anchor after top-roping a route, you call down to your belayer to "Take!" your weight. The rope comes taut, and you will be hanging from the two quickdraws, which are clipped to two separate anchor bolts, and which you now need to clean.

The first step is to go off belay, but before you can consider yourself safely off belay, you must clip yourself directly to the anchor using *redundancy*. "Redundancy" means that you aren't relying on just one piece of gear to keep you safe. If one bolt or carabiner fails, there are others to back you up. (That isn't to say that carabiners or bolts fail simply by weighting them, but the concept of redundancy protects even a worst-case scenario.)

To clip yourself to an anchor with redundancy, you'll need two quickdraws. First, clip both quickdraws to your belay loop. Now take the second carabiner of one draw and clip it to the bottom carabiner of the anchor quickdraw (the one you are going to clean). Do the same with the other quickdraws. (See figure 4-10, step 2.)

Ideally you want to be clipped in direct

99

in such a way that your harness is *below* the lower-off point, which is the part of the anchor that is the rounded (i.e., not sharp) surface of a quicklink or ring.

Tying a knot to your belay loop. With two quickdraws clipped in direct to the two separate anchor bolts, you are technically safely off belay. However, since you are planning to be lowered by your belayer, there is no need to give the "Off belay" command to the belayer. Just say that you need "Slack!" Your belayer pays out about 10 feet of slack; he does not take you off belay, and the rope is not unclipped from the Grigri.

Pull up 5 feet of slack; now tie a figure eight on a bight in the rope. Clip the knot to your belay loop with the small locking carabiner you keep on your harness. (See step 3 in figure 4-10.)

Threading the rope through the anchor. Untie your knot completely. Thread the rope through the anchor's lower-off point or points. (See step 4 in figure 4-10.) Double-check to make sure you have correctly threaded the rope through the metal loop or loops.

Going back on belay. After threading the rope through the anchor, tie back in to the rope end using your main knot. (See step 5A in figure 4-10.)

Untie the figure eight on a bight from the locking carabiner on your harness. (See step 5B in figure 4-10.) Call down to your belayer to "Take!"

A great belayer will ask you to *triple-check* that your knot is properly tied, and to make sure the rope is safely running through the anchors. After checking, tell your belayer that your knot has been checked and looks good. At this point your belayer will take in all of the rope. Wait to feel that your belayer has your weight fully. Don't do anything until you hear the audible confirmation from your belayer that "I have you!"

Cleaning the anchor. Lowering down. Once you have physical and audible confirmation that things are in order, it's safe to unclip yourself from the anchors by unclipping the quickdraw tethers from your belay loop. Clean your gear by unclipping it from the anchor and placing it on your harness gear loops. Once you've retrieved your gear, call down to your belayer, "Lower, please!" (See step 6 in figure 4-10.)

THE TWELVE TENETS OF SAFE SPORT CLIMBING

1) Wear a helmet, even for belaying. Bad lead falls and falling rocks have injured or killed both climbers and belayers.
2) Once you begin to tie your tie-in knot, don't stop until you are finished. Avoid distractions, even talking. It's okay to ask people to be quiet when you are tying your knot. Likewise it's polite not to talk to climbers who are tying their knots.
3) Before anyone leaves the ground, always double-check these five things: climber's harness is doubled back, climber's knot is tied, belayer's harness is doubled back, belay device is loaded, belay carabiner is locked.
4) Always tie a knot into the end of your rope.
5) Never grab for gear to prevent a fall. Just let the fall happen; the rope will catch you.
6) Never put your finger through a bolt hanger!
7) Never lower through just a nylon sling—rope goes on metal only! Also never lower through just a bolt hanger. When in doubt, leave your own carabiners—you can usually retrieve them later.
8) Communicate loudly and clearly. Good communication begins on the ground.
9) Always use your partner's name, especially at crowded crags. "Yes, you are on belay, Chris Sharma!"
10) Take care of your rope. Inspect it for damage to the core every time you flake it. Trim damaged ends. Know how long your rope is.
11) Never untie your knot unless you are safely clipped into two points.
12) Never clean your draws on rappel—always have the belayer lower you as you clean, or clean them on top rope.

Remain vigilant to safety. Remember to KISS. When feeling bold or reckless, check yourself and return to that state of safety consciousness.

CHAPTER 5

Chuck Fryberger enjoys the warm air and tranquil setting of South Africa while leading a 5.13a arête. (Photo © Keith Ladzinski)

Taking the Sharp End: Leading a Sport Climb

Leading is exciting. High on a wall, the wind whipping at the back of your neck, and a bit too runout to feel much at ease, you will experience some of your most memorable moments on what is called the "sharp end" of the rope. Leading is the main goal in sport climbing: we do it to overcome the true difficulties of the rock and the mental knots in our heads. It's at once satisfying and thrilling.

Leading never ceases to be at least a little intimidating. The fears associated with falling and failure are hurdles every single climber will face, not just as a beginner but throughout his or her career in the sport. This is part of the game. Some days it will be easier, and some frustratingly harder. The key is not to beat yourself up too much, but instead to identify your weaknesses and fears, and to systematically and patiently tackle them one at a time. Do this, and one day you may wake up and realize that not only is falling a lot of fun, but that you are climbing longer, steeper, and harder routes than you ever imagined.

But before getting ahead of yourself, take the time to learn how to lead climbs that are below your free-climbing abilities. The basic progression for most sport climbers can be broken down into three distinct phases:

Phase 1: Learn the free-climbing skills and ropework techniques that will keep you and your partners safe: how to belay, give a soft catch, clean anchors, and be savvy to all the other smaller safety issues of climbing outside. Begin with top-roping—push yourself on top rope to see where you're at grade-wise. Flesh out your arsenal of free-climbing moves. Become comfortable with the gear—see that it works and learn to trust it.

Phase 2: When you're ready, try leading a well-protected (not too runout) sport climb that is easy for you. Learn the art of leading and falling, and work on this until you reach a point where you are comfortable onsight leading sport climbs of grades at or below your top-roping level.

Phase 3: Finally, begin to push yourself by leading routes of increasingly higher grades, eventually working on redpointing a single project that's very difficult for you. This is the biggest and most important step, the point in your career when you feel confident enough in your ability that you will say goodbye to top-roping and hop on the sharp end without ever looking back. Reaching this point is ultimately the most liberating feeling in sport climbing because you will have opened up the entire world of bolted routes. There are tens of thousands out there waiting for you to enjoy.

ANATOMY OF A SPORT CLIMB

Length. Sport climbs differ greatly in length—they can be as short as 20 feet and as long as 250 feet. Typically sport climbs are 60–100 feet (20–30 meters). There will be bolts about every 3 to 12 feet up a sport climb, and a two-bolt anchor at its end.

Belay box. This is the area at the base of the route where the belayer stands. The size of the belay box is only constrained by whether there are trees, bushes, cliffs, or other belayers in the area. Otherwise, the belayer uses a large (about 10 x 10 feet) space at the base of the route.

Crux. The crux is a free-climbing sequence that makes up the route's hardest moves. Usually the difficulty of a crux is what determines the rating of the rock climb. Sometimes it's easy to see where the crux is from the ground, but not always. The relatively blanker, steeper sections of any rock climb are often cruxes, but it's hard to be sure until you get up there and check them out. Holds can be hidden, and occasionally the hardest-looking sections turn out to be the easiest.

Many climbers struggle to grasp how the technical difficulty of a single crux translates to the overall rating of a route. Ratings are not an exact science, but there is some logic to how routes are rated. Sport climbs can be graded for their single hardest move, and they can also be graded for the overall difficulty (linking together every move). Usually it's the shorter sport climbs that are graded by the difficulty of a single crux move or sequence. Longer routes require *fitness*—not just endurance, but the endurance to pull a crux at the top of the route.

For example, imagine two 100-foot routes. If the first route has a 5.12a crux right at the bottom, then a pretty good rest, and then follows 5.10 terrain to the top, then the route would be rated 5.12a.

Let's say the second route has the same 5.10 difficulties for the first 90 feet of the climb. Now, instead of a rest, you slap the exact same 5.12a crux from the first route

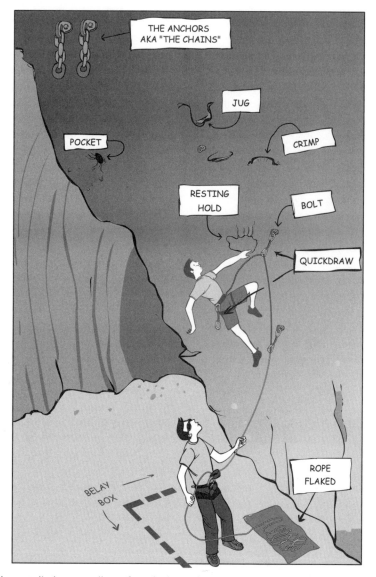

Fig. 5-1. All sport climbs, regardless of grade, have the same essential components. There are bolts for clipping quickdraws, holds for free climbing, and an anchor at the end of the route, allowing you to lower down and safely retrieve your gear.

to the very top of this one. Even though the crux moves of these two routes are exactly the same, due to their position on the climbs relative to the other moves, it's likely these routes would be given different grades. The second route would probably be rated harder, perhaps 5.12b.

Cruxes are usually relative: different climbers will find different sections troubling. Shorter climbers may be frustrated finding they must do more, often harder moves to surmount sections that taller climbers have no trouble with at all; conversely, taller climbers may not be able to do the "scrunchy moves" that fit short climbers perfectly.

Sometimes, there are no particularly hard (or easy) parts, and the crux of the route is simply getting to the top before your forearms fail.

Redpoint crux. This odd term is derived from the fact that people fall on moves *above* what is generally considered to be the route's main (or "technical") crux. The redpoint crux doesn't have the hardest moves on the route—but rather, the moves are still hard enough to cause a fall.

When working a route—hanging, falling, and resting your way up it—redpoint cruxes aren't always apparent. The moves may feel easy after resting on a bolt, but when you have to do them after climbing the prior moves in succession, they feel much more difficult than they really are. Hence, it is the crux of the redpoint.

Tickmark. This is a dab or line of chalk intentionally placed to indicate where a hold is—or often where the best part of a hold

is. Tickmarks may also indicate hard-to-see footholds. Any well-traveled route will have unintentional tickmarks—residual chalk on the wall from prior ascents—indicating where the holds are. Many footholds are scuffed by black shoe rubber. Use chalk markings to help you find holds, but don't get tunnel vision. Look for hand- or footholds that aren't chalked up or covered in boot rubber that may suit you better.

Tickmarks are placed after falling during the process of working out a viable sequence. Use tickmarks sparingly. It's better style to not place tickmarks, plus relying on your memory will actually make you a better free climber. Don't ever tick every single hold! If you do *need* to place one or two tickmarks, always brush them off after you have sent the route.

THE REAL DEAL: OUT OF THE GYM AND OUT TO THE CRAG

These days most people are introduced to climbing in a gym. Modern climbing gyms are excellent places to learn proper belay technique and hone the fundamentals of free climbing. The walls of most gyms are also equipped with fixcd quickdraws to practice leading.

Sport climbing areas are as close to a gym as you can get outside, though the differences are vast when it comes to the important stuff like safety. Sport climbers must be completely self-reliant and responsible for their actions. This begins with knowing the basics of how to belay a leader, and extends to knowing how to evaluate the integrity of your own gear as well as the gear that's fixed on the wall, knowing how to avoid loose rock, and responding appropriately to bad weather, especially lightning. Be aware of these crucial points:

Don't assume fixed gear is reliable. In a gym, setters and managers make sure that the ropes are in top condition, that bolts are properly tightened, and that top ropes are safely strung. There's no manager of outdoor sport-climbing areas, and it's up to the experienced members of any climbing community to take action and replace fixed hardware that has become dangerous.

Bad bolts are a legitimate concern as the earliest routes enter their third decade. However, at most areas, especially on popular routes, older bolts have been replaced with $1/2$-inch, five-piece expansion bolts, which are plenty solid. Look at the bolt's nut: Is it securely threaded on the bolt, or is it about to unscrew itself? Is the hanger loose? Is the bolt rusted? Is there a gap between the bolt/hanger and the rock itself? These things indicate a dubious, if not downright dangerous, bolt.

A more common concern is the integrity of fixed quickdraws that have been hanging on routes, perhaps for years. Be wary of faded nylon, and always check the basket of every carabiner you clip to see if its edge is sharp. Never rely on a sharp or badly worn carabiner—replace it with your own newer one.

Outdoor climbing areas are dangerous. Rocks fall, people drop gear, and bad weather moves in. Wear a helmet, even for belaying. Dress properly and always be prepared for the cold and rain.

Not all routes are safe! Not all route developers know what they are doing. Sometimes loose rock hasn't been properly cleaned, or the route takes you up a sketchy flake that could pull out at any moment. Threats such as this one could potentially injure your belayer or cut your rope. Sometimes developers mistakenly place bolts in such a way that your rope runs over/around a sharp corner or edge. Though the route developer may be to blame, it's your responsibility to recognize dangerous situations and avoid them. Bail off any climb you think is dangerous—there are plenty of good, safe, and enjoyable sport routes out there.

Route vs. rope length. Lowering a climber off the end of the rope is never a concern in the gym, but it is outside. A full 60-meter (200-foot) rope will get you up and down 90 percent of the sport climbs in the United States, but don't assume that it will. Consult guidebooks and other climbers about a route's length. If a route is 30 meters long, you need *at least* a 60-meter rope! And whatever you do, always tie a knot in the end of the rope.

Gym climbing is not sport climbing. With the plethora of training apparatuses like tread walls, system boards, hang boards, and campus boards, you can get ridiculously strong in a climbing gym. However, that strength doesn't always transfer directly to sport climbing. Standing on plastic footholds and following a taped route on a wooden wall will not fully prepare you

Fig. 5-2. Wilderness crags like Acephale, tucked away in Canada's beautiful Bow Valley, present many objective dangers not found in the gym. Here, Joe Kinder fires Endless Summer (5.13d).

for climbing on real rock. Here are a few reasons why:

Real rock can be sharp and painful. Your skin may be callused, but if it's only accustomed to grabbing plastic holds, you may find that your skin gives out before your muscles do. If this happens, make sure you take care of your skin that night by rubbing vitamin E oil into your fingertips and moisturizing. Skin with more moisture has more water in it, which makes it stronger. Dry, cracked skin tears easier. Lightly file down calluses and any raised tissue that could catch on a sharp nubbin and tear off.

People set gym routes; rock is natural. This is obvious, but the point is that rock climbs demand moves that you've never seen or practiced before. Rock climbs are more three-dimensional than gym routes. Prepare to be frustrated, stymied, and more pumped than you think you should be.

Sport climbing may feel scarier. People are instinctually afraid of anything unfamiliar. If you've only climbed in the gym, you might find climbing outside to be a bit headier. Don't worry about it; this is natural. Relax, breathe, and drop the tension from your shoulders. The more you do it, the easier it will be.

THE BIG LEAGUES: FROM BOULDERING TO SPORT CLIMBING

As a boulderer you've had plenty of experience in the gym, and you've put in your days outside "wrestling pebbles." You have a pretty solid background in free climbing—especially with working hard, powerful moves—and now you want to tie in for the long ride.

The biggest mistake boulderers make when getting into sport climbing is thinking that an ability to pull hard moves automatically translates into knowing how to safely lead and be a great belayer. Actually, it's often other sport climbers who blindly make this assumption about you, making it even harder to be honest about your experience. Climb with proficient sport climbers and don't shy away from asking questions.

Don't get ahead of yourself. Take the time to safely learn how to navigate a sport climb. Spend time leading easier routes and build up the confidence to be on the sharp end. Start with shorter routes and work up to the longer ones.

Also, take the time needed to become a great belayer. You should be able to give soft catches to partners of all different weights. Learn how to clean routes, especially the overhanging ones.

The biggest challenge, however, will be changing how you free climb. In bouldering, the name of the game is *crushing every hold* until you reach the top. Try to do that on a sport route, and *you* will get crushed. Sport climbing is all about learning to let go, while still hanging on.

A NEW DIRECTION: GOING FROM TRAD TO SPORT

Trad climbing is exponentially more complicated than sport climbing in terms of leading and gear. Basic trad climbing skills include properly setting cams and nuts so they will hold a fall and not pull out when the rope jostles them; placing gear that avoids rope drag; building an anchor and equalizing it; routefinding; and belay escape and self-rescue.

One would assume that with a solid background in gear and rope management, trad climbers would easily transition into sport climbing. In some ways, it's true—yet trad climbers, like everyone else, do face a learning curve.

Different gear. Most trad climbers use ATCs, thick ropes (or double ropes), and shoulder-length slings that have been doubled to make ersatz quickdraws. Eventually you'll find that standard quickdraws are more durable and easier to grab, and that an ATC is not as useful as a Grigri for belaying.

Lowering, not rappelling, off a route. You rarely lower your partner in trad climbing. Skills such as cleaning quickdraws on the lower, especially on really steep climbs, will be difficult.

Take pro where it is. You don't get to pick and choose where your pieces go. Even though sport climbs are safe, many trad climbers are surprised by how runout the climbing can be.

Fear of falling. Pitching off the wall is less frequent in trad climbing because the consequences are often more serious. Fear of falling is sometimes crippling to trad climbers just getting into sport climbing. It's not just the fear itself that's the problem— it's the resultant hesitation to *go for it* that stifles one's progress most.

Better belaying. Because falls are less common in trad climbing, there's typically less expertise in knowing how to catch them. Trad climbers, no matter how experienced, will usually need to spend some time learning belaying skills such as giving a soft catch, holding a hangdogging climber's weight, belaying a climber who needs to "boink," and helping a climber who's cleaning draws stay trammed into the line when lowering.

Increased difficulty. It can be a bit shocking to discover how much more difficult the free-climbing moves are in sport climbing. Even great trad climbers with "good heads" for leading can feel uncomfortable pulling on tiny holds and making big dynamic moves above their last quickdraw.

MOVING FROM TOP-ROPING TO LEADING

Though top-roping is a great way to learn how to rock climb, you don't want to get too comfortable doing it because you'll never lead anything. On the other hand, leading is not something to rush into. Even a well-bolted sport climb presents inexperienced leaders many opportunities to hurt themselves if they don't know how to fall, or if they aren't strong enough to hang from one arm long enough to clip the rope through the quickdraw...or any number of things.

No one who's never done it before is ever really "ready" to lead. That's because no matter how well you "know what to do," the actual experience of taking the sharp end will inevitably be different. You will screw up and climb with the rope behind your leg as surely as you will accidentally backclip a quickdraw because you're pumped stupid. Most common, the good, smooth, and relaxed climbing technique that you have on top rope will suddenly disappear as soon as you're standing well above the last quickdraw and well below the next one.

Leading is more complicated and scarier than top-roping—it changes how you free climb, even though in theory it shouldn't. The sooner you can get off the top ropes and onto the sharp end, the better you will become, quicker.

It can be easy to avoid pushing yourself on lead, especially if you—like most beginners—climb with a partner who is better or more experienced than you. It takes a bit of willpower and a lot of commitment to hop on lead when it's something you find uncomfortable. There are no real shortcuts to gaining and maintaining this motivation. One good trick is to pull the rope down once your partner gets down on the ground—before you can think about it too much, remove the option to top-rope.

COMMANDING LANGUAGE: HOW TO TALK TO YOUR BELAYER

Before you take the sharp end, make sure you (and your belayer) understand these standard commands. It's always best to be as descriptive as possible. Don't simply say, "Okay," if someone asks whether he is on belay. Repeat the question in the affirmative: "Yes, you are on belay!" It's better to keep negatives short and clear: "No, you are NOT!"

Also, to avoid confusion always use your partner's name, especially when other people are around. "You are on belay, Angelina!"

"Up rope!" There is too much slack in a top-rope situation. *Response:* The belayer takes in more rope until the rope is almost taut, but not so much that the climber is pulled off balance.

"Take!" The climber wants the belayer to hold his entire weight. *Response:* Quickly but safely the belayer takes in all slack and sits back on the rope, holding the climber's weight.

"Slack!" Two definitions: If the climber is on lead, it means the rope is too tight. If the climber is clipped in direct to a bolt or at the anchor, it means the climber needs slack to either clip up to a higher bolt or to thread the anchor. *Response:* Belayer gives out one big loop of slack and waits to see if climber needs more.

"Clipping!" The leader is about to pull up slack quickly to clip a quickdraw. *Response:* The belayer gives out two big loops of slack.

"Watch me!" The leader is feeling insecure and feels like he may fall. *Response:* The belayer should be watching the leader anyway, but it's nice for the belayer to give an audible response that is positive and comforting such as, "I'm with you, *homie!*" or "You got it, *girl!*"

"Falling!" The climber is about to fall. *Response:* If the climber is on top rope, the belayer should lean back on the rope to take in as much slack as possible. If the climber is on lead, the belayer should get into an athletic stance and prepare to give a soft catch (see chapter 8).

"I'm in direct." The climber has used a quickdraw to clip his harness directly to a bolt. *Response:* The belayer can let out a foot of slack and relax, using this time to stretch the neck or sip water. Because the climber is not off belay, but only in direct, the belayer still holds the rope with the brake hand.

"Off belay!" The climber is safely clipped in to two bolts at an anchor and is preparing to clean the anchor and retrieve the quickdraws. *Response:* The belayer gives out about 10 feet of cord. With single-pitch sport routes where the climber is lowered, the belayer should not unclip the rope from the belay device.

"On you!" Two uses: After being in direct to a bolt, the climber is ready to unclip his dogging draw, and he would now like to be held by the rope (belayer). Or if the climber is at an anchor, the climber has finished cleaning an anchor and would like the belayer to take. *Response:* The belayer takes in all the rope until the climber's weight is fully held, and says, "OK, I have you!"

"Lower!" The climber would like to be

FLAKING THE ROPE

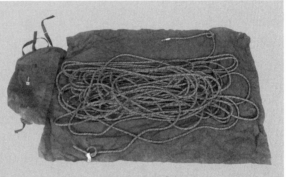

Always "flake the rope" at the base of any route you're going to do. This simply means running the rope through your hands from one end to the other, making a neat and manageable pile of cord on top of your rope bag's tarp. If you don't have a rope bag, flake your rope onto a pack or large flat stone—anything to keep it out of the dirt.

Flaking the rope gives you a chance to feel your cord and to inspect it for any damage. Feel for soft spots with your fingers, and check the sheath for fraying or cuts.

A properly flaked rope will not tie itself into a knot or kink up during a belay. The last thing the belayer needs is to deal with a badly kinked rope. The more you flake your rope, the less kinked it will be.

A good tip for flaking is to make the bottom coils large, and each consecutive one slightly smaller. This prevents a rope from tying itself into a knot.

Make a habit of switching which end you climb on—whether you switch the end between each route, or at the start of each new day at the crag. This prolongs rope life and keeps your cord from getting kinked.

lowered, but not all the way to the ground. *Response:* The belayer lowers the climber slowly until the climber yells, "Stop!" The belayer then holds the climber's weight and awaits the next command.

"Dirt me!" The climber would like to be lowered all the way to the ground. *Response:* The belayer lowers the climber to the ground at a steady pace.

"Rock!" The climber has knocked off a rock or ripped a hold off the wall. *Response:* Belayer should move close to the wall and "get small." The belayer should not look up!

THE LEADING PRIMER

Upon choosing a route that you are going to lead, you will take the following steps:

1) Flake your rope onto your rope bag beneath the climb's first quickdraw.
2) Put your harness on; make sure it's doubled back.
3) Check that your rope is long enough to get you up and down the route. Do you have enough draws, including two for the anchor (and not including your one dogging draw)? Choose the number of draws you will need and rack them on your harness.
4) Survey the climb. What parts look hard? Are there any runouts to prepare for? If so, instruct your belayer to "Watch me" on those sections. Do you want to stick clip the first bolt? (See chapter 7 for how to stick clip.)

5) Put your shoes on. Make sure you have enough chalk.
6) Tie your knot. Have your belayer put you on belay.
7) Double check the knot, harnesses, belay device, and belay carabiner—visually and with dialogue.
8) Climb on!

RACKING QUICKDRAWS ON YOUR HARNESS

There are certain categories in life that, while ultimately pointless, are eternally fascinating because of how perfectly they divide people into two camps. There are those people who wave to strangers when they drive, and those who don't. Some people arrange their toilet paper so it feeds from the bottom of the roll, while others want the opposite. In sport climbing, the great divider is whether you prefer to rack quickdraws on your harness with the gates facing in or out.

Both have benefits, and ultimately it doesn't really matter which method you choose. Pick one and stick with it. Personally, I prefer the gate facing in toward my body because I can simply open the gate and lift the draw *up* from my harness. You might disagree with me and that just means we play for different teams. The point is that you want to get fast at taking a draw off your harness and clipping it to a bolt.

Remember that every quickdraw has one

Fig. 5-3. Ben Rueck climbs up to the first clip of a 5.9, Mill Creek, Utah.

top carabiner and one bottom carabiner. These carabiners are NOT interchangeable, so it's your job to make sure they don't get mixed up. (See "Quickdraws," chapter 3.) Most companies sell quickdraws with two completely different carabiners on each quickdraw.

Always clip the *top carabiner* of the quickdraw to the gear loop of your harness. This way, when you unclip the top carabiner from your harness, it's already in your hand and ready to be attached to a bolt. The number of draws you bring depends on how long the route is. The best guidebooks tell you the number of quickdraws you need to bring for a particular route, but otherwise you can try to count the number of bolts from the ground. You need one quickdraw for every bolt, plus two for the anchors (unless the anchors have fixed carabiners). This tally shouldn't count the one lightweight dogging draw that you keep on your harness at all times. Ten to twelve quickdraws will get you up and down most sport climbs. Rack the draws evenly on either side of your harness (e.g., five quickdraws on each side).

CLIPPING QUICKDRAWS TO BOLTS

When you see a bolt hanger above you, look around for good-looking holds to clip from (they are usually the ones with lots of chalk on them). Is there a hold below or above the bolt that looks good enough to hang from one-handed?

Take the time needed to find a good stance. Don't rush or panic. Never grab the bolt hanger with your hand! You could lose a finger if you fall. Furthermore, if you're grabbing the bolt hanger with a finger, how are you going to clip the quickdraw to it?

Find the position that gives you total balance between your feet and the hand you're going to hang from in order to clip. Stay poised and focus on even, relaxed breathing. Although it may seem awful in the moment, the worst that can happen is that you fall.

Take one quickdraw from your harness, and clip the top carabiner to the bolt hanger so that the gate faces the *opposite* direction of where the climb trends. Look ahead: Do the upcoming holds take you to the right or to the left? If you can't tell, look for the next bolt: Is it up and left, or up and right of where you are?

Clipping the quickdraw the wrong way—so that the top carabiner's gate is facing *toward* the upcoming direction of your travel—is potentially dangerous if the rope shifts the quickdraw into a horizontal position, in which the gate is more likely to press against the bolt nut or the bolt hanger, potentially unclipping itself in a fall. With the gate facing down and away from the hanger/bolt, it's in no danger of pushing against it and coming unclipped.

A draw unclipping itself from a bolt hanger is rather rare. It has only happened to me once, and I've heard of it happening about five or so times, never resulting in an injury. Still, the potential for something bad to happen is there, so clip correctly.

Also beware of hangers that have shifted, or ones that spin, because they can cause quickdraws to sit funny.

Cross-clipping. In some instances you may need to break out a technique called "cross-clipping," which is clipping a draw/bolt that's to one side of your body using the hand on the opposite side. As a general rule you want to avoid cross-clipping as it may throw you out of balance during the very crucial moment of clipping the rope to your gear. Cross-clipping also tends to be more strenuous. However, it's also true that in some situations cross-clipping can be more efficient than matching on a hold, or making another move to a potentially worse hold. It's a good technique to use when you're in a tight spot, but look around first for a better hold or body position.

Pulling up slack. Now that you've placed the quickdraw on the bolt, the next step is to clip the rope through its bottom carabiner.

- First, call down "Clipping!" to your belayer. If a quickdraw is above or level with your head, you will typically need to pull up the rope *twice*.
- Reach down and grab the rope about a foot away from your knot.
- Pull it up to your mouth and bite the rope lightly with the tips of your front teeth.
- Reach down again and grab the rope. Once you have this second loop of rope in your hand, immediately drop the rope out of your mouth.

Fig. 5-4. Cross-clipping is sometimes more efficient. Here, the climber would have had to make a difficult match; instead he just crossed under and clipped. (Photo © David Clifford)

Fig. 5-5. Bring the rope to your mouth, bite it, then pull up more rope to clip an overhead draw.

This should be more than enough slack to get you clipped to the next draw. Pull the rope up and clip it to the bottom carabiner, but keep the following things in mind.

By the skin of your teeth. A friend of mine lost her two front teeth when she fell mid-clip with the rope in her mouth. If possible it is better to avoid using your mouth at all. Try pulling up slack by cradling the rope with an upward-facing open palm and simply lifting your arm up to the bottom carabiner of the quickdraw. As you pull the rope up, it will run over your hand. This technique can be more strenuous, especially if your belayer accidentally hoses you for slack. It is also slower. This technique works best when the quickdraw is at chest or waist height. Most climbers use a combination of both techniques.

The dangers of "clipping slack." By introducing these extra 3 or so feet of "clipping slack," you are exposing yourself to a much longer fall if you blow it before getting the rope into the carabiner. Falling with this clipping slack will add at least 6 feet to the fall.

For example, imagine you are 5 feet above the last bolt (which, with no clipping slack out, would result in a 10-foot fall). If you pull up clipping slack here and fall before successfully clipping, depending on rope stretch you could be looking at a 16–20 footer! Especially at the second and third bolts of a route, falling with clipping slack out could mean hitting the ground.

The safer technique is to climb further up and clip the quickdraw at your waist by simply reaching to the side and snapping the rope through. Though you have climbed higher, you won't fall as far as you would from lower down with a lot of clipping slack.

The bottom line. Ultimately the safest clipping technique is to find a body position in which you are stable, balanced, strong, and secure. You should feel confident that you won't fall unexpectedly when pulling up a lot of slack to clip the second draw. Sure, if you fell, you could hit the ground— but you are in a position where you *know* you won't.

This is the art of leading: constantly remaining aware of the consequences, responding to stimuli in your body (knowing whether you're too pumped to clip or not), and managing the risk by executing the proper action.

CLIPPING THE ROPE TO THE QUICKDRAW

There are distinctly right and wrong ways to clip the rope to the quickdraw. Correctly clipping a quickdraw involves placing the rope into the carabiner so that the rope leading to the climber comes out through the front side of the carabiner, the side facing away from the wall. The wrong way is called "backclipping," and it's the opposite: the rope leading to the climber comes out the "back side" of the carabiner, which is the side facing the rock. (See figure 5-6.)

It's easy to mistake a backclipped quickdraw for a correctly clipped one if the quickdraw's dogbone becomes twisted around 180 degrees, as it tends to do when

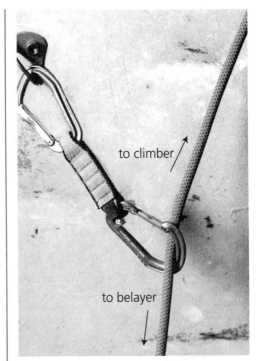

Fig. 5-6. A backclipped draw: the rope comes "out" of the carabiner on the wall side. This is wrong.

backclipped. The lead end of the rope appears to be coming out of the front side of the carabiner only because the dogbone is twisted; however, the quickdraw is still backclipped. A backclipped quickdraw is dangerous because there is a chance of the rope unclipping itself from the carabiner in a fall. In figure 5-7 the side of the rope leading to the climber is about to come taut on the biner's gate and press it open. The rope will no longer be clipped to the quickdraw.

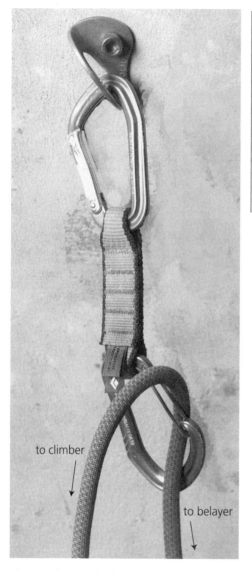

There are two or three basic hand motions climbers use to quickly clip the rope to a draw. This is a skill worth mastering before you start leading, and you can do so by simply hanging a draw at home and practicing with your rope.

The snap clip. Use this motion when the carabiner gate faces the opposite direction of the hand you want to use (i.e., gate facing right, left hand; gate facing left, right hand). I call this the snap clip because doing it quickly almost feels like snapping your fingers.

Fig. 5-7. The rope is about to push the gate open and unclip itself, showing how a back-clipped draw is dangerous.

Fig. 5-8. Snap clip

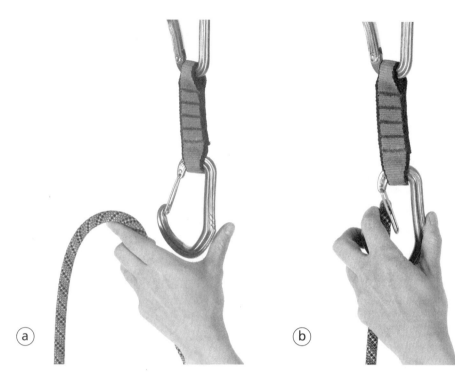

Fig. 5-9. Pinch clip

▨ Grab the rope between your thumb and pointer finger.
▨ Hold the quickdraw steady by placing the tip of your middle finger in the carabiner basket. (See figure 5-8.)
▨ Use your thumb to propel the rope through the carabiner gate. Snap it in!
▨ Don't let the rope fall onto and trap your fingers.

The pinch clip. Use this motion when the carabiner gate faces the same direction as the hand you want to use (i.e., gate facing right, right hand; gate facing left, left hand).

▨ Grab the rope by "hooking" your pointer and middle fingers underneath it.
▨ Place your thumb on the exterior of the carabiner's spine. (See figure 5-9a.)
▨ Pinch the rope through the carabiner gate by squeezing your thumb and fingers together. However, don't push your pointer and middle fingers all the way through the gate—you just want to push hard enough to let the rope fall into the carabiner basket. (See figure 5-9b.)

The reverse pinch clip. This motion is another way to clip in situations when you'd use the Snap Clip (i.e., gate facing left, right hand; gate facing right, left hand), only the fingers and thumb play opposite roles.

- Grab the rope by hooking it with the crook of your hand between the thumb and pointer finger. In this scenario, your palm faces up toward the sky.
- Hold the exterior of the carabiner spine with your four fingers. (See figure 5-10.)
- Push the rope through the carabiner using your thumb and the meat of your hand.

Fig. 5-10. Reverse pinch clip

ABC'S OF THE Z-CLIP

After backclipping, the second most common way to incorrectly clip the quickdraw to the bolt is something called the Z-clip, which happens when the leader grabs slack from *below* the lower quickdraw and brings it up, clipping the rope to the higher one.

This error in clipping gets its name because the rope forms a sideways Z shape: the rope goes down from the climber to the lower draw, back up into the higher draw, then back down to the belayer. (See figure 5-11.) You'll know you've Z-clipped as soon as you try to move up and can't go anywhere.

Z-clipping happens only when the bolts are close together. A surefire way to prevent Z-clipping is to grab the rope near your knot and pull up slack from there.

MANAGING THE ROPE AS YOU LEAD

As soon as you step above the last quickdraw, you must be conscious of two things:
1) The rope's position in relation to your leg.
2) Your leg's position in relation to the rope and the lower quickdraw.

You don't want the rope running *behind* your leg. If sport routes climbed like ladders, you'd never have to worry about getting the rope behind your leg; however, free climbing is intricate, and you will inevitably be bringing your leg across your body in order to backstep, high-step, or traverse left or right.

If you fall with the rope behind your leg, you will be flipped upside-down when the rope comes taut and pushes your leg out from under you! Many climbers have been injured this way, and the upside-down nature of the fall makes head injuries likely. This is one of the many reasons it's a good idea to wear a foam helmet.

When you find yourself above and right of a bolt, the rope should run to the outside of your left foot. Likewise, if you're above and left of a bolt, the rope should run to the outside of your right foot.

In either example, as soon as you move back to the plumb line, directly above the last bolt, you'll want the rope running between your legs.

Never cross your leg between the rope and the wall, and if you do so by accident, fix it before doing anything else.

CLIPPING QUICKDRAWS TO THE ANCHOR

Hooray, you reached the top of a sport climb! Now you have to get down.

If the anchors have clippable fixed lowering gear, you simply clip the rope to both anchors and lower.

If your partner wants to top-rope the climb, or you are going to try the route again, or there is no fixed lowering gear, you need to place two of your own quickdraws.

Clip each quickdraw directly to each bolt hanger, if possible. If the anchors are the type that will need to be cleaned, don't clip the quickdraws to the lower-off point.

Fig. 5-11. Climber has mistakenly Z-clipped the rope, and is now unable to move upward.

Fig. 5-12. Wrong! The rope is "behind the leg" of the climber. The climber should swing her left leg around so the rope is running between her legs

If the bolts are staggered, it's okay to clip one quickdraw to a chain link and the other to the bolt hanger. Ideally the bottom carabiners of both quickdraws will be even with one another as shown in figure 5-13.

Finally, clip the quickdraws to the anchor such that the gates of the bottom carabiners face opposite directions.

Style. When you get to redpointing (see chapter 10) you may find it's hard to clip both the anchors. You've climbed the whole route, you're pumped, and you're in a rush to get the rope through the carabiners so you can say, "Take!" Because clipping the anchors is hard, some sport climbers have employed dubious tactics that raise questions about what counts and what doesn't.

Do you need to clip *both* quickdraws? Can you call it "good" if you only clip one quickdraw at the anchor and then crumple onto the rope? Most climbers say yes. Clip one for the send and two for safety!

Extending anchors is invalid. Some climbers add extended slings or draws to make clipping the anchors easier from a few moves below the top of the route. I've seen some truly egregious situations where climbers have added *10 feet* of webbing to an anchor in order to clip from lower. It's okay to extend the anchor by the length of one quickdraw, but any longer is getting into questionable territory. If you decide it's necessary to extend the anchors, you must at least climb the last few moves to the top of the route to claim an ascent.

Fig. 5-13. A typical anchor. Two draws have been clipped, one to the lower bolt hanger, the other to a chain link so that the bottom carabiners are even with each other. Always top-rope through your own gear.

Falling after clipping. If you get the rope through both anchor quickdraws, but then fall . . . congratulations, it still counts!

125

CHAPTER 6

Kleman Becan taking the 60-foot joyride at Oliana, Spain (Photo © Keith Ladzinski)

The Art of Falling

"You need to have a section in your book about how climbers *need* to get over their fear of falling," advised my friend Ethan Pringle, one of our country's top sport climbers. "I think that is the number-one factor holding people back from achieving their potential and learning to have fun!"

It's funny that climbers have such great difficulty with what in some ways is the "easiest" part of the entire sport-climbing experience. Falling is inevitable—it happens without consent or permission. Doing it is simply a matter of letting go—gravity will take care of the rest.

However, falling is no laughing matter. In bad (but fortunately rare) cases, climbers break ankles and crack bones in lead falls. In most instances, however, falling simply means you did not send the climb. It's not the worst thing in the world, even though it

sometimes feels that way at the time.

Despite negative associations, falling is actually a positive thing. Pitching off a route signifies that you are trying something that is hard for you. Good. When you fall, take it as evidence that you are on the right track to improving.

A trad-climbing fall is complicated by two factors: how you physically manage the fall, and whether your gear holds. The presence of reliable fixed protection—bolts—in sport climbing strips the fall down to just one of those things: the technique of maneuvering through the air and bracing yourself for any potential impact. Falling is a basic climbing technique that is best learned on sport climbs, and that will directly transfer over to all other roped disciplines.

Yet falling is not so much a *technique* to

Fig. 6-1. The author doing what he does best: falling off of a crux (Photo © David Clifford)

be learned as it is an art form to be mastered. The art of falling draws on experience, combined with some intuition and a lot of good reflexes.

Needless to say, none of it will matter unless you have a great belayer. In that sense, staying safe in a fall is totally out of your hands. There's not much you can do if your belayer drops you or, as happens more commonly, gives you a hard catch that slams you into the wall—though it is possible to minimize the impact of a hard catch with good falling technique. The first step to proper falling is to climb with people who are great belayers, to be one yourself (see chapter 8), and to be confident in your ability to fall safely.

TAKING THE WHIPPER 101

Don't push away. Rather, gently drop off. The harder you push away from the wall, the harder you will come back into it.

Don't grab anything. Don't grab quickdraws, or lurch for rock holds, or try to hold yourself by grabbing the other end of the rope. Let the gear do its job. Even if you are only two feet above the last bolt, don't dive for the quickdraw. Trying to "catch" yourself is a good way to lose fingers, get rope burns, or dislocate your shoulder.

The exception to this is when the bolt is at your waist or you are one foot above it; then it's okay to reach down and grab the quickdraw as long as you do it *with control.*

Call to your belayer to "Take!" and when you feel the rope come taut, let go. You don't want to drop down onto your arm. Grab the draw, wait until your belayer takes your weight, then drop off the rock.

Stay calm. Don't flail around. If you are relaxed and limber you are less likely to get injured.

Spot your impact zone. Right before you fall try to visualize where you will be stopping. If you're directly above your bolt, look for any ledges/protrusions/roofs directly below you. Falling above and off to either side of the bolt will cause you to swing down across the rock face like a pendulum, though rope stretch will significantly dampen the arc of your swing. Spot your landing. If you are up and left of the bolt, look down and to its right—and vice versa. Spot any dangerous protrusions, corners, or blocks and plan on meeting them with your legs bent and limber. You may not be able to avoid hitting the problematic feature, but being aware of it may help you minimize the damage.

Keep the spring in your step. Imagine jumping off a boulder to the ground: your legs are bent and prepared to absorb the impact. A sport-climbing fall is similar, only you want to sit in your harness and keep your legs out in front of you. That way, your feet will hit the wall first and your legs will absorb the impact. However, don't stick your legs out so far that your body becomes horizontal. Keep your torso upright, sit in your harness, and keep your legs out in front of you and ready for impact.

Hands to yourself. Avoid using your hands to stop yourself from slamming into the wall—you could sprain your wrist.

Communicate. If you are about to fall, alert your belayer with a loud and clear "Falling!" so he can get into an athletic stance for a soft catch. Don't make the common error of saying "Take!" before you fall. Telling your belayer to take in all the slack is precisely what you don't want because it may result in a hard catch that *will* hurt.

Just fall. Let it happen. Don't fight gravity. It's okay to fall in sport climbing. The more falls you take, the more comfortable you will become with it. The more comfortable you are, the more focused you will be on the actual climbing, which is what this is all about.

WHEN IT'S NOT OKAY TO FALL

On almost every sport climb, there are certain situations when the old trad-climber adage "The leader shall not fall" applies. The three most common ones are:

At the second bolt. Arriving at the second bolt, and especially clipping it, momentarily puts you in a precarious position—blowing the second clip would more than likely send you to the ground from rather far up. Take special care with this crucial bolt. If reaching the second bolt is very hard, consider stick clipping it from the ground (see chapter 7). If you're sketching out getting to the second bolt, consider

downclimbing a few moves to a safer stance and recomposing yourself.

While clipping. Pulling up slack to clip an overhead quickdraw elongates the fall potential greatly; and pulling up slack to clip the second bolt is usually the most dangerous thing you'll do on lead. Leaders safely navigate this risk by finding good,

Fig. 6-2. Grab a quickdraw by the dogbone, clip the rope to the carabiner, and say, "Take."

solid stances, and by knowing their limitations. It also helps to be adept at clipping the rope to the quickdraw quickly. If you feel like you aren't going to complete a clip after having pulled up all that slack, just drop the rope and grab the quickdraw's dogbone. (See figure 6-2.) Hang onto the draw, get the rope through the carabiner, and tell your belayer to "Take!"

With the rope behind your leg. You do not want to fall with your leg behind the rope because it will flip you upside down and cause you to smash into the wall. Wearing a helmet could help protect your head from an injury here. If you're not wearing a helmet, and you fall with the rope behind your leg, place both hands on the back of your head for protection and try to do a sit-up. Curling up into a sit-up position will keep your head and neck better protected.

MASTERING THE FALLING MENTALITY

Good falling technique begins well before you even fall. Leading isn't just about reading the rock and executing the moves. Part of the game is staying aware of the consequences. Ask yourself, "What would happen to me *if* I fell right now?"

Understand that if you traverse off to the left of a quickdraw, a fall would send you swinging down to the right like a pendulum. Are there protrusions off to the right that might cause injury? How far is that ledge beneath you? Is it something you might hit if you fall from a few moves higher? If so, how do the upcoming moves look? If they look easy, maybe the ledge beneath you isn't such a big deal.

The ultimate goal is to be constantly answering these kinds of questions, but—here's the catch—you must do it *without consciously thinking about it.*

Thinking about falling when climbing is a self-fulfilling prophecy without comparison. You want to be *completely aware* without ever having that internal dialogue creep into your head, which should be totally focused on reading the rock and executing the moves to get up the climb—efficiently, cleanly, perfectly.

Ultimately, the myriad incarnations of the fall you *could* take will play in your head like white noise. A great leader has a trained ear that responds to the particular notes of alarm, but is otherwise capable of tuning out the rest in order to focus on climbing well. This is a state of mind that is best achieved through experience, and even then it's not guaranteed.

RATIONAL VS. IRRATIONAL FEARS

It's completely natural to be afraid of falling... even onto a perfectly safe bolt. I don't know any climbers who *aren't* afraid of falling to some degree. This fear is not something you will ever "overcome" either,

Fig. 6-3. Nathan Welton, on a 5.12d at Penitente Canyon, Colorado, showing what can happen if you fall with the rope behind your leg (Photo © Amy Mann)

nor should you. Fear is an important circuit hardwired into our brains that tells us to avoid dangerous situations.

Fear becomes a problem when it stifles our progress and performance in situations where no danger exists. Most of the time, falling on a sport climb is safe, and the fears we have are more irrational than grounded in reality. The first step to managing any fear is to deconstruct it and thus understand it. Fear in climbing breaks down into two categories: rational fears and irrational fears.

Rational fear is an appropriate response to true danger, while an irrational fear is unjustified because no true danger exists. The term "irrational fear" should not be taken as an affront toward your feelings; it's not meant to trivialize the very real, gripping sensation you feel when faced with a sport-climbing fall. These terms are non-judgmental, and are meant to be descriptive terms that help us define, categorize, and label that which scares us. The more we understand who we are and how our world works, the less fearful we become.

Good gear, proper ropework technique, safe belaying, and solid bolts almost eliminate any real reason to be afraid in sport climbing. The clearest example of an irrational fear limiting us is the apprehension many climbers feel as they stare up at a steep, overhanging rock climb. In fact, the steeper sport routes may be the safest of all since there is little chance of slamming back into the rock and getting hurt. We find steep routes intimidating because

the moves look hard, increasing the chance that we *will* take a fall. But if the bolts are solid and closely spaced, falling off a steep climb is just a matter of dropping a few feet through the air until the belayer catches you. The fear of falling through air is irrational since there is very little real danger.

CONFRONTING FEAR AND WORKING THROUGH IT

Fear, like a 5.13 rock climb, is a nebulous, massive, incomprehensible thing at first. However, as you will learn in chapter 10, "Redpointing," the key to tackling any monumental challenge—whether it's learning how to overcome your fear of falling, or redpointing your first 5.13—is to break it down into easily digestible pieces. Here are some tips to do that.

Expand your comfort zone a bit every day. If you have a desire to improve, this is one of the most important concepts you need to learn. The "comfort zone" is a space that's relative to each and every climber, but it is universally a place where we feel comfortable operating. It's the status quo, a figurative bubble where things are safe and familiar.

The dangerous thing about a comfort zone is that it's a perpetually shrinking space. The longer we stay inside it, the smaller it gets. The more habitual we make our lives, the less elastic we become and the harder it is to improve and expand. In other words, the more we choose to top-rope routes because we're afraid of leading them, the harder it will become to actually lead. The more quickdraws we grab and the more falls we avoid, the harder it will be to learn to climb through the fatigue. That's not to suggest that we never top-rope or never grab quickdraws—the point is that we need to actually *work* at making those weak moments the exceptions, not the rules.

Why? Because staying in our comfort zones prevents us from discovering (and often being surprised by) the sometimes amazing things we are capable of accomplishing, whether it's leading a 5.11 for the first time or skipping a pumpy clip en route to redpointing the hardest route of our lives.

Climbers who seem like they never get scared are an illusion. Their comfort zones may be larger than yours, but they feel the same as you do when pushed outside it. That said, pushing yourself outside of the comfort zone definitely becomes easier as you do it more. Over time you'll notice you have less apprehension about tackling the next bigger thing when you've built that foundation of many small but hardly insignificant successes.

Make a vow, right now, to expand your comfort zone at least once every time you go out climbing. Push yourself in some way to face your own irrational fears. Try leading one hard route above your head. Take the dreaded fall on your project that you've thus far avoided by grabbing a draw. Climb one extra pitch at the end of every day, even if it means falling because you're tired.

But certainly don't make the whole day an exercise in being scared. If we did that every time we went out climbing, we'd never have any fun. Most importantly sport climbing is meant to be fun. Top-rope some good climbs, laugh and holler when you get to the top, and practice your *Thriller* dance when you get back to the ground. Then, maybe try one of the comfort-zone-expanding exercises listed below. And always finish the day on a good, happy note by doing something that makes you laugh.

Learn to fall in the gym. A gym is a fantastic place to become accustomed to the sensation of dropping off of a wall into air. There are usually no objective dangers such as corners, blocks or ledges for you to hit. Also, you can get a sense of how much ropes will stretch, and the confidence that your belayer will catch you. However, be aware how different falling in the gym is compared to the real thing—it's arguably safer and certainly less intimidating. It's a good place to learn the most stripped-down fundamentals, but not much else. Take the experience with a grain of salt.

Use a top rope. If you're afraid of getting on lead, ask your partners to set up a situation so that you can top-rope a route while practicing leading. You need two ropes to do this, and two belayers: one person will belay you with a loose top rope, while the other person will belay you on lead. You will climb up, clipping the lead rope through the quickdraws, while the top rope will be there to alleviate your fear. Try taking a little lead fall. Learn to trust the gear. It really works.

Clip and fall. Pick a route within your free-climbing abilities, preferably one that you have done before on top rope. Stick clip the first or second quickdraw, then lead the rest of the route. Practice making clips quickly. After each clip, take a fall. Don't tell your belayer to "Take!" Just say, "Falling!" and let go. Do this with each quickdraw until you get to the top.

Take a whipper. Some people learn best by jumping into the deep end. Find a nice steep, safe route that is within your leading abilities, and take a big fall. Climb up to the last draw, and instead of clipping it climb one or two more moves above it and fall. See that whipping into space is perfectly safe.

REGAINING YOUR HIGH POINT AFTER A FALL

YARDING UP THE ROPE

So, you've taken the whipper and you're at the figurative and literal end of your rope. The aftermath of any fall involves uncomfortable sensations: you're likely physically exhausted, perhaps still feeling a bit scared, and, in general, are feeling defeated. However, don't let the route get the best of you. Now is the time to get back on the climb and figure out the moves. But how?

Depending on the steepness of the wall, and the direction of the route line, you will need to employ one, or a combination, of various tactics—which range from easy to difficult—that will allow you to regain the high quickdraw.

After falling you will want to regain your high point. Yarding up the rope simply means winching yourself up the rope by pulling down on the belayer's side of the rope.

Falling usually means you are extremely pumped—you may need to rest on the end of the rope for a minute before yarding up the climb.

Before yarding, look down to your belayer and ask if he is ready. Upon getting the go-ahead, grab the belayer's side of the rope and begin winching yourself, hand-over-hand, up the rope. (See figure 6-5.) The upper quickdraw acts as a pulley and with the full weight of your belayer on the other end, you shouldn't find yarding up the rope to be too taxing, especially if your belayer is heavier than you are.

Yarding will be easier on you if you work with your belayer, using his weight as much as possible to help pull you up. Make only one yard at a time, and keep in sync with your belayer. Wait for the belayer to jump up the rope so his full weight is helping to

GOOD STYLE: DON'T BE *THAT GUY!*

When some climbers fall they get angry and start yarding up the rope instantly, before the belayer is ready. Slow down, buddy! Your belayer just caught you—give him the time needed to settle into a solid position. Don't start yarding until your belayer says you can.

Fig. 6-4. Jessa Younker drinks in the aftermath of a fall on Techno Christ *(5.12c), Mill Creek, Utah.*
(Photo © David Clifford)

pull you up. Look for footholds that you can use to push yourself up while pulling down with your arms.

When you reach your high point, take your dogging draw and go in direct to the quickdraw. Take a breather, scope the moves, brush holds, and visualize yourself getting through the next section.

YARDING ON A STEEP/ TRAVERSING ROUTE

Yarding up the rope on a steep route is more complicated because you may have trouble reaching the belayer's end of the rope if you are dangling out in space. When you fall on the steepest climbs, you may swing in toward the belayer's end of the rope. If you do, try to snag it and hold yourself there for a second by wrapping your leg around the rope. Or you can use your dogging draw to tram into the line.

If you can't reach the belayer's end of the rope, there are three last-ditch techniques you can try before "boinking" (explained below):

Push off the rock. Use your legs to push off the rock and generate the momentum to swing over to the rope. The key to doing this successfully is totally counterintuitive: *Push yourself in the opposite direction of where you want to go.* Push yourself *away* from the belayer's end of the rope, and you will subsequently swing in toward it.

Pump the swing. Remember "pumping" a playground swing as a child? You build momentum by shifting/sliding your center of gravity around to a natural rhythm. If you can get yourself going by pushing off the rock as described above, you can give two or three pumps like you're on a swing, which is usually enough to enable you to reach out and grab the belayer's end of the rope.

Snap it with a quickdraw. If the rope is *just* out of your reach, try using your dogging draw to help you span the last few inches. Hold one of the dogging draw's carabiners in one hand and flick the quickdraw's other carabiner at the rope, trying to "snap" it through.

BOINKING

On the steepest climbs, a fall strands you out in space, leaving you dangling helplessly at the end of your rope. If you can't reach the rope to yard up then you must resort to "boinking."

Boinking means pulling yourself up the rope and letting go at the acme of your upward pull—this creates a moment of weightlessness, which allows the belayer to absorb all the slack. You move up, while your belayer drops down.

Does that sound hard? Unfortunately, if you're not strong it might be. But with a little practice and good body awareness, even those who can't do a single pull-up can boink. Here's how:

1) Wait for your belayer to "jump up the rope" a couple of times so their entire

Fig. 6-5. Yarding: pull hand-over-hand, using your belayer's counterweight to help you up.

Fig. 6-6. When stranded in space, boinking helps you regain the rock.

Fig. 6-7. Boinking employs the belayer's counterweight to inch you up the rope

weight is hanging on the line. (See chapter 8 for how to belay the boink.)

1) Grab the rope with both hands. Lean all the way back on your arms. Swing your legs back and forth two times to get a little momentum going.

2) Here comes the crux: pull down hard on the rope while simultaneously kicking your legs straight up into the air. (See figure 6-7.) Imagine an Olympic high jumper doing the Fosbury Flop, arching their back headfirst over a bar, then

Fig. 6-8. By pulling yourself up the rope, you create a moment of weightlessness that is absorbed by the belayer's weight.

kicking their legs over it as well. Boinking is almost exactly like the Fosbury Flop, only it's in reverse: you lead the motion with your feet first!

3) At the acme of your pull, as your legs begin to come down from their kick,

let go of the rope. This sudden release in tension creates a weightless moment that sends your belayer dropping down/back a few inches to a foot. (See figure 6-8.)

4) If you've boinked correctly, you will be

Fig. 6-9. Walking the rope requires flexibility, but it can be easier than boinking.

Fig. 6-10. Walking the rope: put one foot on the rope.

a few inches higher, while your belayer will be a few inches lower.

Repeat this process until you can reach the belayer's side of the rope and yard up it. Keep in mind that boinking may not work if you are more than 60 pounds heavier than your belayer.

WALKING THE ROPE

If boinking doesn't work, your only other option is to "walk the rope," a technique that requires a fair bit of flexibility and balance. Walking the rope is more dangerous than boinking because if you screw up and fall there's a chance you could get a limb

Fig. 6-11. Walking the rope: reach for a quickdraw.

tangled up in the cord. Your safety relies on the sturdiness of your position on the line. Here's how to walk the rope:

1) Tell your belayer to get into a stable position on the ground, still holding your weight. Also, clip your dogging draw to your belay loop, so it's ready to go.

2) Grab the rope with one hand, and lean back a bit. Use your other hand to pull one foot up *onto the rope.* This is the hardest part, especially if you're not flexible.

3) Begin pushing down on the rope with your foot while simultaneously pulling your upper body up the rope using your hands. (See figure 6-10.)

4) Pull yourself up until you have one foot standing on the rope.

5) Reach for a quickdraw or the other end of the rope, grab it, and alert your belayer that you're about to unweight the rope. (See figure 6-11.) It's important to be in sync with your belayer here. Hold the quickdraw firmly, and walk your feet onto the wall/rock. Take your dogging draw to clip in direct.

Your belayer will take up all the remaining slack, and you will be back on the route.

CHAPTER 7

Amanda Berezowski fires up the fun, athletic moves of Jingus (5.12d), Acephale, Canada.
(Photo © Keith Ladzinski)

Advanced Ropework Techniques for Leading and Cleaning

The scene was a little painful to watch. For over an hour a climber was utterly stymied by the clip of a 5.11's crux section. The first half of the route is forgettable, while the second half, after the crux, is a brilliant corner with fun moves.

After resting on the draw, the climber would summon the gumption to make it to the next bolt. After two moves, he would reach up and desperately try to clip a quickdraw to the hanger, but his poor, unbalanced body position kept him from reaching it. When his strength faded, he'd either downclimb or take a little fall onto the bolt at his waist.

To make matters worse, between each of these attempts, he rested for five or more minutes on the rope, relegating his belayer—who probably weighed 60 pounds less than he did—to holding him.

The climber finally gave up. He clipped a carabiner to his high-point bolt and lowered, retrieving his draws. Because of the difficult clip, he never made it past the crux and missed out on the best part of the route. Though this climber did nothing overtly wrong, his ignorance about ropework foiled his success.

His biggest mistake was letting his fear of falling prevent him from finding a good clipping stance. The fall would have been safe, but he was so fixated on hanging the next draw that his basic free-climbing technique suffered. One mark of a good leader is learning to relax in gripping situations. You have to train the calm, rational part of your consciousness to block the panicky, irrational part that perpetually attempts to seize control when things get a little uncomfortable.

That aside, this climber simply didn't

know the ropework techniques that would have helped him get the next draw hanging. With it clipped, he could have easily pulled through the crux—or worked out the moves—and then climbed on to the anchor. Also, he never went in direct, burdening his poor belayer. Last but not least, because he never reached the anchor, his belayer—who wanted to top-rope the route—never got a chance to climb.

On new routes, especially harder projects, it's common that you won't be able to make clips or figure out the crux sequence on the first attempt. Fortunately, a savvy climber who knows how to hangdog, go in direct, clip up with a stick clip, or clip up by hand can usually get up and down any sport climb, regardless of its difficulty.

This is wonderful news for those looking to safely push their boundaries and comfort zones. In traditional climbing we are correctly taught to exhibit more prudence when jumping to a new grade. In sport climbing it's okay to get on a route that's above your head—in fact that's the name of the game.

STICK CLIPPING

Do you stick clip the first bolt or not? Put it this way: it's never a *bad* idea.

Stick clipping has a stigma for some. I remember belaying my friend at our local crag one day when a sponsored climber with a well-deserved reputation for bold, traditional ascents showed up to try a 5.13a adjacent to us. The route is an area classic,

but it has a hard start—in fact, some holds have broken on it—which is why people stick clip the first bolt. For 15 minutes he pulled onto the rock, tried to find a hold, and fell back down. Since he was new to the area, I explained that stick clipping the first bolt on this particular route is standard, but he barked: "I *don't* stick clip!"

"Suit yourself," I said. The climber never even made it off the ground—eventually he packed up his rope and left. The saddest thing of all is that his pride prevented him from going climbing.

If the start of the route looks hard—or you're simply nervous about reaching the first bolt safely—by all means use a stick clip! Sport climbing is about minimizing danger in order to enjoy the movement of the route.

STICK CLIPPING A QUICKDRAW TO A BOLT

Whether you're using a spring clamp stick clip or a Superclip, the basic process for clipping draw to bolt or rope to draw is the same.

1) Extend the telescopic pole of your stick clip all the way.
2) Take the quickdraw in your hand, and, facing the wall, orient it in front of you so that the top carabiner is facing away from the direction you will be climbing once above the bolt.
3) Flake out about 10 or 15 feet from the end of the rope, and clip it to the bottom carabiner of the quickdraw so that it's not backclipped in this orientation.
4) *With a spring clamp stick clip:* Open the

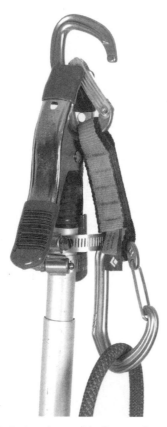

Fig. 7-1. Spring clamp stick clip—ready to clip a quickdraw to a bolt hanger

Fig. 7-2. The Superclip prongs hold the top gate open, allowing you to hook the carabiner to a bolt hanger overhead.

top carabiner of the quickdraw fully, so the gate is touching the carabiner spine. Open the spring clamp and clamp down on the point where the carabiner gate and spine touch. Clamping the gate to the spine keeps the carabiner open. *With the Superclip:* Simply push the top carabiner through the metal "goal posts" so that the gate stays open.

5) While holding the pole, bring the quickdraw up to the bolt. Hook the top carabiner through the bolt hanger. Again, make sure the orientation of the draw is proper.

6) Once the carabiner is through the bolt hanger (see figure 7-3), pull down on the pole until the spring clamp (or Super-clip) disengages. Olé!

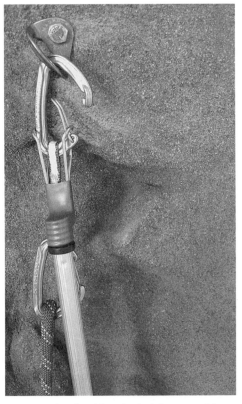

Fig. 7-3. *After hooking the bolt hanger with the quickdraw, just pull the stick and the Superclip will release from the quickdraw.*

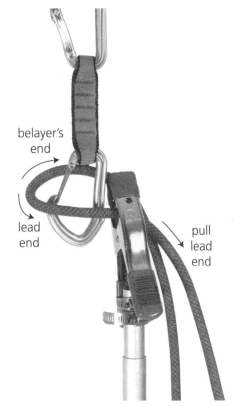

belayer's end

lead end

pull lead end

Fig. 7-4. *Clipping the rope to a pre-hanging quickdraw using a spring clamp stick clip*

STICK CLIPPING THE ROPE THROUGH A PRE-HANGING QUICKDRAW

First, look up and take note of which way the bottom carabiner's gate is facing: right or left?

With a spring clamp stick clip:

1) Starting with the climber's side of the rope, flake out enough line to reach the quickdraw.

2) Make a loop (bight) of rope about three inches in diameter. You want the bight to be *just* big enough to pass a carabiner through it. Facing the wall, hold the bight in front of you so it's standing up in the air, perpendicular to the rock. The lead end is on the side of the bight closest to you.

If the bottom carabiner's gate is on the left, fold the bight 90 degrees to the left. If the gate faces right, fold the bight down to the right.

3) Clamp down at the base of the bight such that the belayer's side/strand is more securely clamped than the lead end. Make sure you don't lose the orientation you just created in the bight. You want the lead end on the side closest to you in order to prevent backclipping.

4) Raise the pole up to the quickdraw. Finagle the bight of rope so it "lassos" the bottom carabiner. The bight of rope is touching the carabiner gate, and the stick clip is against the carabiner's spine.

5) Pull the lead end of the rope. As you pull, the loop of rope will get smaller, eventually pinching down on the carabiner gate and clipping itself through. (See figure 7-4.) Done correctly, your rope won't be backclipped.

6) Hold both ends of the rope and pull the spring clamp down/off the rope.

With the Superclip:

Follow the first three steps above, then continue:

4) Take the bight of rope and wedge it between the two goal posts of the Superclip.

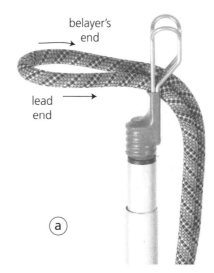

belayer's end

lead end

(a)

Fig. 7-5. Clipping the rope to a pre-hanging quickdraw with the Superclip

---

GOOD STYLE: STICK CLIPPING RULES

While stick clipping is legitimate, if it gets taken too far it can invalidate an ascent. Stick clipping the third bolt or higher creates a top rope for a significant portion of a climb—and while top-roping is okay, it doesn't count as a true lead.

I've also seen climbers lead halfway up a route and then lower to the ground to rest, leaving the rope strung through the first four or five bolts. When they are ready, they sprint up the first half of the route, which supposedly saves them the energy they'll need to make it to the top. This scheme, however, is also invalid. It's perfectly fine to practice moves with the safety of a top rope, but at some point you will have to climb the route with no more than the first quickdraw stick clipped for the ascent to count.

(b)

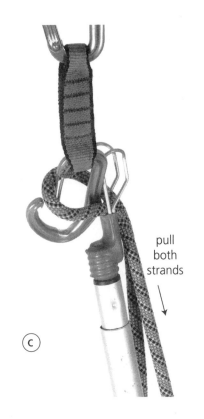

(c)

pull
both
strands

5) Hold the pole up and lasso the bight around the bottom carabiner. (See figure 7-5b.)

6) Gently pull *both* strands of rope down to pinch the carabiner gate and clip the rope through. (See figure 7-5c.)

HOW TO RODEO CLIP

Rodeo clipping is the Hail Mary pass of stick clipping. Lacking a real stick clip, you can try your hand at whipping a loop of rope into the first quickdraw, which is about as difficult as it sounds.

For rodeo clipping to work, the bottom carabiner of the first draw needs to be hanging away from the wall—it can't be flat against the rock.

1) Stand perpendicular to the wall, directly beneath the gate-side of the carabiner.

2) Take a loop of rope in one hand and begin whirling it around in circles to the side of your body. Adjust the radius of the circles by letting out a bit of rope at a time until the apex of the rope's arc is even with the bottom carabiner.

3) Now that you've got your height adjusted,

begin aiming the whirling rope at the carabiner's gate. If you're lucky (or talented), you will not only snap the loop through the carabiner's gate, but the rope won't be backclipped. If you get it on your first try, take it as a sign that you're going to send.

ON ROUTE: CLIPPING UP

The crossover in techniques between aid climbing and sport climbing is surprising because we usually think of the two disciplines as polar opposites. However, everything is connected in climbing, and there's no reason to shun one discipline when learning from it could make you a better climber.

It is often possible to clip the next bolt from the one you are at by getting into the classic aid-climber "top-step" stance. The climber from this chapter's introductory anecdote could've easily clipped the route's crux bolt by "clipping up." Any time you are hangdogging a route, working out the moves, or just trying to get the draws hung, look for spots where it will be possible to clip up. Having the next draw hung and clipped will help you find hidden handholds, decipher crux sequences, and pull through moves you can't do yet.

To clip up, first go in direct. Ask your belayer for slack. (See figure 7-6.)

Place your feet high on good footholds and push upward with your legs. Due to the tether created by the dogging draw, the upward force of your legs causes you to

Fig. 7-6. After going in direct, pull up slack to clip up.

Fig. 7-7. Use your feet to push yourself up, steadying yourself with a grip on the draw at your waist. Clip up.

pivot around the bolt like a compass.

It may help to grab the dogging draw with one hand as you stand up to stabilize yourself. Otherwise, use any holds on the wall for stability—pull down on a hold while driving yourself up with your legs to reach really high. (See figure 7-7.)

This stance is surprisingly taxing, especially on your legs and core (abs and lower back). You may only be able to be fully upright for a few seconds, which is why you want to execute the next steps quickly.

If there is no quickdraw above you, reach up and clip one to the bolt hanger. Pull up an arm's length of rope and clip into the quickdraw.

If the next bolt/draw is still just out of reach, try one of the following tips:

Go in direct to the *top carabiner* of the hanging draw, or better yet, the bolt hanger itself. This may give you three or more inches of reach.

If you can find a stable stem or stance, or reach a good hold up higher, you can also try to *lengthen* your tether/dogging draw by using two dogging draws chained together and clipped to the route draw. With a longer tether, it's harder to actually get up, so you will definitely need to use a clever body position using the rock holds. Having a longer tether will allow you to climb up higher, but be careful: you *don't* want to fall onto your draws because the fall will be "static" and possibly injurious to your back.

You can also make a ladder rung by chaining two to four quickdraws together. Clip the rung to the bolt, and you now have a step to stand in that may give you the extra height you need to clip up.

After successfully clipping up, come back down with control so you are once again hanging on your dogging draw. Don't just drop off, because you will take a static fall.

Ask your belayer to "Take." Unclip your dogging draw. Either yard up the rope to the next bolt, or climb up there with the benefit of the next draw already clipped.

THE COWBOY CLIP UP

When the next draw is already hanging but you can't reach it to clip up, it may be possible to rodeo clip it from your position at the lower bolt. For the technique to even have a chance, the target quickdraw must not be flat against the wall.

Go in direct. Ask your belayer for slack. Estimate the length of slack it'll take to reach the quickdraw overhead. If it's 5 feet above you, you'll need to pull up 10 feet of slack to create a 5-foot loop.

With the loop, take a practice swing at the carabiner to see if you have the right length. Make adjustments—you want the apex of the rope to perfectly hit the bull's eye: the center of the carabiner's gate.

Being in direct, you can't swing the rope around in circles like you can when rodeo clipping from the ground. Instead whip the loop across the plane of the face, like a giant windshield wiper, aiming to snag the bight through the carabiner's gate on that one pass. When you miss, you'll have to place the loop back on the other side of your body and try again.

If you successfully rodeo clip the draw,

but it's backclipped, that's okay. Tell your belayer, "On you!" Unclip your dogging draw. Yard up the rope. Now, go in direct to the upper draw and fix the rope so it's not backclipped.

CALLING UP THE STICK CLIP

If you can't clip up, cowboy-style or regularly, you can "call up the stick clip."

The safest way to get a stick clip up to your high point is to lower down to the ground, clip the stick clip to the back of your harness, and then climb/hangdog/ yard your way back up to your high point on top rope. I suggest doing this if the route is short, or if you are only a third of the way up. Once you've regained your high point, go in direct, pull up the slack you'll need, and stick clip the next bolt.

The other method many sport climbers employ is *not safe*. Still, it's the standard procedure you see used at crags all over the world. It involves going in direct to a single bolt, and going off belay; the climber then pulls up a lot of slack in order to lower a giant loop to the ground. The belayer next clips the stick clip into the loop of rope, and the climber pulls it up. Once the climber has the stick clip, the belayer pulls down all of the slack and puts the climber back on belay.

The reason this method is *not safe* is because it breaks a basic safety rule—that you should never trust your life to a single anchor point. Should that one bolt fail in the above scenario, the climber would plummet to the ground. Most bolts are solid, and it's highly unlikely that a good bolt will ever pull out of its hole. However, bolts have failed in the past, which means they will fail in the future. Never trust your life to a single bolt if you can help it.

It is possible, however, to perform this procedure described above and also be safely clipped into two bolts. Upon reaching your high point and realizing you need/want the stick clip, call down "Take" to your belayer. Then say "Lower." Perform the following steps.

1) Lower down to the bolt just below you, and go in direct with your dogging draw.

2) Grab the belayer's end of the rope and pull up enough slack to tie a figure eight on a bight into the line. Clip the knot to your belay loop with the small locking carabiner you always carry with you.

3) Now you are clipped to two bolts—the higher one via the loop of rope, and the lower one via the dogging draw. It's now safe to go off belay.

4) After your belayer takes you off belay, pull up enough slack to lower a giant loop of rope, to which your belayer can clip the stick clip. (See figure 7-9.)

5) Pull up the stick clip (figure 7-10) and clip it to your harness. Wait for your belayer to take in all of the line and put you back on belay. You're not on belay until you have audible confirmation from your belayer.

6) Untie the figure eight on a bight. Call down "Take" and when you feel the belayer is once again holding your

Fig. 7-8. This climber is clipped in direct to the bolt in front of him. He is using the rope to secure himself to the bolt above him by tying a figure eight on a bight, and clipping it to his harness via a locking carabiner. He is attached to two bolts, and can now be considered safely off belay.

Fig. 7-9. Calling up the stick clip: lower a giant loop of rope to your belayer.

Fig. 7-10. Calling up the stick clip: pull up the stick clip and attach it to your harness.

Fig. 7-11. Calling up the stick clip: yard up the rope.

Fig. 7-12. Calling up the stick clip: pull up a loop of rope.

Fig. 7-13. Stick clipping an overhead quickdraw

weight, unclip your dogging draw from the lower bolt.

7) Yard up the rope (figure 7-11) to your high point and go in direct again. You are now in place to stick clip the next bolt or quickdraw. Pull up a loop of rope, enough to reach the next quickdraw or bolt. (See figure 7-12.) Stick clip the next bolt. After stick clipping the bolt, toss the stick clip down into a bush or onto a tree branch. Or, clip the stick clip to the bolt and leave it there while you climb the remaining half of the route. Retrieve it when you lower down.

CLEANING A ROUTE: RETRIEVING QUICKDRAWS

Retrieving your quickdraws involves a technique called "cleaning the route." On slabs and vertical faces that don't traverse, cleaning the route is simple. On steep walls or traversing routes, cleaning can feel more difficult than the actual climbing!

Upon reaching the anchor, assess the situation. Do you need to clean the anchor first? (See chapter 4.) If you don't need to clean the anchor, check the integrity of the fixed lowering gear. Are the carabiners sharp or worn? If so, replace them. You're about to trust your life to the anchor, so make sure everything is solid.

On vertical or slabby routes, here's the basic technique you'll need to retrieve your quickdraws on the lower.

1) After cleaning the anchor or clipping the fixed carabiners, take your dogging draw and tram in to the belayer's side

Fig. 7-14. Use your dogging draw to tram in to the belayer's side of the rope when cleaning. Here, the climber stops just above the draw she wants to retrieve.

of the rope: clip one end of the draw to your belay loop, and the other end to the belayer's side of the rope.

2) Instruct your belayer to "Lower, please!" You will be slowly lowered down the route, with the dogging draw sliding down the rope with you. The dogging draw acts as a tram that will bring you right to each of the route's quickdraws so you can easily remove them.

3) Just before you reach the quickdraw, instruct your belayer to "Stop!" You don't want to ever be lowered *below* the quickdraw you want to clean, so stop early. Your belayer holds your weight while you clean: don't unclip your dogging draw from the rope. Unclip the bolt-hanger side of the quickdraw first. After you unclip the quickdraw from the bolt hanger, unclip it from the rope; now rack it on your harness. Instruct your belayer to "Lower, please!"

4) The first bolt is the crux of cleaning a route, requiring you to coordinate with your belayer and pay attention to any swing out from the wall that you may take.

    Most importantly, never remain trammed in to the belayer's end of the rope after having cleaned every quickdraw! This is important because if you swing out away from the wall, you could drag your belayer through the dirt with you, possibly injuring him.

5) Upon reaching the first bolt—which is the last quickdraw to be cleaned—unclip your dogging draw from the belayer's side of the rope, and use it to go in direct

Fig. 7-15. At the first bolt, the climber has gone in direct and is unclipping belayer's end so that the belayer can take in all of the excess slack.

to the first quickdraw of the route.

6) Now unclip the belayer's side of the rope from the first quickdraw. With you in direct, your belayer can move out of your way if you should swing out.

7) Tell your belayer to "Take."

8) When your belayer has you, hold the rock and unclip the first quickdraw from the bolt hanger. You may swing out from the wall. Then, your belayer will lower you to the ground. When you touch down and find your footing, say, "I'm off belay!"

CLEANING A STEEP/ TRAVERSING ROUTE

Stripping the draws on a steep, overhanging rock climb is by no means easy. It also presents many more complications—such as swinging out like a pendulum once you clean the route's first quickdraw. Swinging out can be fun, but it's also dangerous in certain settings. Many sport climbers have sustained bad puncture wounds when they've swung out into a grove of trees.

Cleaning a steep or traversing route is essentially identical to the basic process described above, but there are a few key differences that mandate subtle changes to the technique of cleaning.

Lowering down and pulling yourself in. Even though you will be trammed in to the belayer's side of the rope, lowering down will put you out in space, far away from the next quickdraw. That's okay. Depending on how far out you are from the wall (i.e., how steep the climb is), you want

to lower down until you are just about level with the quickdraw. On the steepest routes, you will lower until you are a bit below the quickdraw—but only a bit.

When you reach that height, tell your belayer to "Stop!" Your belayer will *lean back hard on the rope*, creating tension in the system that will help pull you toward the wall.

Pull yourself toward the draw by hand-over-handing down the rope. Sometimes it will be easier to invert your entire body to pull yourself in—think of Sylvester Stallone going across the Tyrolean traverse in the opening scene of *Cliffhanger*. (See figure 7-16.)

Hop the dogging draw down. After pulling yourself in, before trying to clean the quickdraw, it usually helps to "hop" your dogging draw so it's below the one you want to clean. Unclip the dogging draw from the line, but then quickly clip it back to the line *beneath the quickdraw*. Don't mess this up because if you somehow don't tram back in to the line, you will swing out and may not be able to finish the job.

Use the rock holds and get ready to swing out. Find a handhold to steady yourself on the wall. To clean the draw, pull yourself into the wall using the handhold while simultaneously unclipping the carabiner from the bolt hanger.

After cleaning the draw and letting go of the rock, you will swing out a bit violently and stop abruptly when your tram catches you from swinging out any farther. Now tell your belayer to continue lowering. Repeat

Fig. 7-16. Cleaning a steep route

this process until you reach the route's *second bolt*.

Manage the swing out. The most important safety concern when cleaning steep routes involves the first quickdraw. Look up at the anchor and imagine an imaginary plumb line coming straight down to the ground. If you were to untram from the belayer's side of the rope, you would

swing out to that imaginary plumb line and then swing past it by an equal distance. Not only that, but as you swing out you will also drop down—again, just like the arc of a pendulum. Scan the environment for any obstacles you could possibly hit. Are there trees that you could hit? Will you sink down low enough to smash into that boulder?

If the answers to these questions are a

Fig. 7-17. Sometimes, it helps to hop your dogging draw underneath the quickdraw you want to clean.

clear-cut "No," you should be fine to clean the first quickdraw as described above. Otherwise, here are some options to help keep you safe:

Clean the first quickdraw from the second bolt. If you're worried about swinging down too low from the first bolt, you can stay higher by cleaning the first quickdraw from the second bolt. To do this, go in direct to the second quickdraw and tell your belayer to give you slack. Reach down and try to unclip the first quickdraw. You may need to invert yourself completely to reach it. After cleaning the first quickdraw, clean the second as if it were the first, following the steps described earlier.

Stay trammed in and leave the first draw clipped. If it's possible to boulder up the wall and easily/safely remove the first quickdraw, leaving the first quickdraw clipped will keep you from swinging out from the wall. Simply stay trammed in to the belayer's side of the rope with your dogging draw and lower down to the ground. Once on the ground, untie and pull the rope. Boulder up to the first clipping hold, retrieve the draw, and downclimb. It's also possible to retrieve the first quickdraw from the ground with the Superclip stick clip.

CONSIDER TOP-ROPING

In some severe situations—if a route traverses more than 50 feet, for example—it will be easier to remove the quickdraws on top rope. This is the safest way to clean quickdraws, but it's also a much bigger pain. Use your judgment.

SO, ARE YOU READY TO LEAD?

Here's a checklist to see if you're ready to lead. Before leading, you should be able to answer a confident "yes" to these questions:

- Do you have a rough idea of what your abilities are, and are you choosing to lead routes within those grades?
- Have you done enough top-roping outdoors to have good sense of what real rock feels like, and what the hand- and footholds look like?
- Do you know the difference between a relaxed, balanced position and a frantic, unbalanced one?
- Do you know how to read rock?

AT THE BASE

- Are you and your belayer on the same page in terms of what the plan is?
- Do you trust your belayer to safely catch any fall you take?
- Is your rope long enough to do the route?
- Do you know all of the commands and what they mean?
- Do you know the five vital checks you must complete before leaving the ground?

ON THE ROUTE

- Do you know how to orient a quickdraw on a bolt hanger?
- Do you know how to pull up slack and clip it to a quickdraw?
- Are you *great* (or just okay) at clipping the rope to a quickdraw? Can you do it with either hand no matter which way the carabiner gate is oriented?

- Do you know how to avoid backclipping?
- Do you know how to grab a quickdraw to make a clip?
- Do you know that you should never grab a bolt hanger?
- Do you know how to evaluate the integrity of fixed gear?

FALLING

- Do you know basic falling technique such as don't push away from the wall and keep your legs braced for impact?

- Do you know when you should *not* fall (e.g., at the second bolt, with the rope behind your leg, with a loop of clipping slack out)?
- Do you know not to grab anything (quickdraws, rope, etc.) when you fall?

AT THE ANCHOR

- Do you know how to clean an anchor?
- Do you know how to clean a route?
- Do you know what to do—and not to do—at the first bolt when cleaning a route?

CHAPTER 8

With the confidence provided by a great belayer, Lauren Lee onsights Windblown Groan *(5.12d), Phalanx of Will, Arizona.* (Photo © Keith Ladzinski)

Great Belaying

Belaying is the system used to catch a falling climber. It also provides a way to hold a climber's weight as well as lower him or her to the ground. Take belaying seriously—your partner's life is literally in your hands.

A great belayer inspires the leader with the confidence to *go for it*. A climber's assurance that he can fall and not get hurt is important for more than just the obvious reasons. The confidence and trust that you will be okay in a fall is necessary to improve free-climbing skills. Climb with people who are great belayers, and reciprocate by being one yourself.

Good belaying means learning the basics—this takes anyone about a day. *Great belaying* means being adept at catching falls long and short with heavier and lighter partners; paying out and taking in slack quickly and safely; making the process of working a route as easy as possible for your partner; and, of course, always being safety conscious.

All climbers could probably belay better than they do, but very few make a point of deliberately improving their belaying skills because they think it's really not that complicated.

Well, that's true. Belaying isn't hard. So why do so many climbers, experienced and inexperienced alike, drop their partners, or lower them off the end of the rope, or give them a "hard catch" that slams them into the wall?

Part of it is just momentary laziness. The other part of it is that great belaying requires mastering the subtleties of the act. It's easy to become inattentive when you're tired or distracted by other people on the ground, or especially when things become repetitive, as they tend to in sport climbing (e.g., you climb with the same person, work the same route, etc.). As a belayer you owe your partner no less than your very best.

This chapter covers how to use a passive/standard device (henceforth ATC) and an autolocking device (henceforth Grigri), and other skills needed for great belaying.

In all cases, this information is not exhaustive, and must be used in conjunction with the instructions provided by the manufacturer of your belay device.

TOP-ROPE VS. LEAD BELAY

Unless you are doing a multipitch sport climb, most of the time you will be on the ground belaying either a top-roping climber or a leader. These two situations require distinct but not dissimilar techniques. The techniques for a top-rope belay are the same with a Grigri and an ATC. A lead belay, however, requires slightly different techniques depending on which device you use.

HOW MUCH ROPE IS "OUT" VS. SLACK IN THE SYSTEM

The amount of rope out is a measure of the distance of rope between the belay device and the climber. The amount of rope out is important because it affects how greatly the rope stretches when weighted. The more rope in the system, the more stretch you can expect in a fall.

TECHNICAL TERMS

Brake hand. Your dominant hand, used to arrest falls and control the speed at which you lower a climber. Don't take your brake hand off the rope. Your brake hand grabs the rope in one of two positions: thumb-toward and thumb-away.

Thumb-toward. In the thumb-toward position, the brake hand is oriented on the rope like it's holding a ski pole—the thumb (as opposed to the pinkie) is "pointing" toward the belay device at all times.

Thumb-away. In the thumb-away position, the pinkie is closest to the belay device, while the thumb points out or away.

Guide hand. Not the brake hand. This hand helps to take in and pay out slack. When lowering with an ATC, the guide hand can assist the brake hand with lowering speed. When lowering with a Grigri, the guide hand operates the lever and controls the speed of descent.

Live end. Think of the belay device as a point that divides the rope into two sides: the live end and the brake end. The live end is the side of the rope that goes to the climber (note: when top-roping, the live end actually goes up through the top anchor and back down to the climber).

Brake end. The side of the rope that goes directly to your brake hand.

Brake position. Whether in the *thumb-away* or *thumb-toward* position, the brake hand is held down to the side of the body, firmly gripping the rope.

With top-roping there is more rope out than with leading because the rope starts at the belay device, goes all the way up to the anchor, then back down to the climber.

How much rope is out is different from how much slack is in the system. The amount of slack is a measure of how far the climber will fall before the rope begins to stretch (become taut) under the weight of the plummeting climber.

The belayer's primary job—with both lead and top-rope belaying—is to adjust how much slack is in the system.

When top-rope belaying, there may be a lot of rope out, but the general rule is to always be minimizing the amount of slack in the system. The belayer does this by constantly taking in rope as the climber ascends.

Lead belayers constantly adjust the amount of slack in the system—paying it out, taking it in. How much slack is out will directly affect how far a lead climber falls. Unlike top-rope belaying, there is no general rule for how much slack there should be in the system. This is one of the main reasons lead belaying is more complex than top-rope belaying.

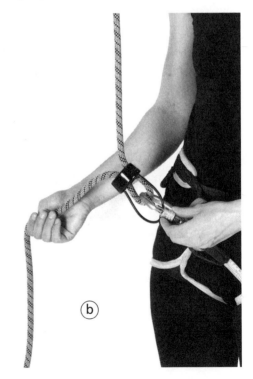

Fig. 8-1. Loading an ATC

LOADING AN ATC

1) Take a bight of rope, pinch it, and push it through a single slit of the ATC. (See figure 8-1a.)
2) Clip a locking carabiner into the bight, between it and the ATC.
3) Clip the locking carabiner (with device/rope) to the belay loop (not the tie-in points) of your harness. Lock the carabiner. (See figure 8-1b.)

LOADING A GRIGRI

1) Clip your locking carabiner to your belay loop (not the tie-in points).
2) Slide the Grigri plate open to reveal its inside. (See figure 8.2a.) Identify the horseshoe-shaped cam in the center—to its left side is a graphic showing a climber; to its right is a graphic showing a brake hand gripping the rope. (These graphics are also pictured on the outer plate.)
3) Lay the rope around the center cam so that it conforms to its horseshoe shape. (See figure 8-2b.) Make sure the live end is on the side with the climber graphic, and the brake end is on the side with the brake-hand graphic. *Getting this backward is a careless and potentially fatal error that will cause the Grigri to not automatically lock up in a fall!*
4) Slide the plate down.
5) Clip the locking carabiner through both holes, now aligned at the edge of the device. Make sure you clip *both holes!*

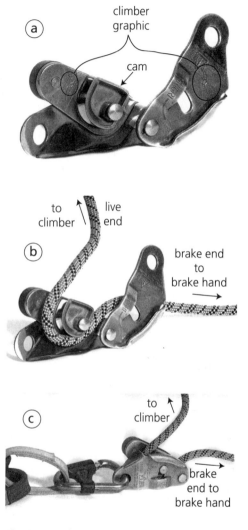

Fig. 8-2. Loading a Grigri

Now, the plate can't slide open.
6) Clip the locker to the belay loop and lock it. (See figure 8-2c.)

HOW DO THE DEVICES WORK?

It's a simple bit of mechanics that a 100-pound climber can catch and hold the weight of a falling 200-pound climber. The more you understand how the devices actually work, the safer you will be.

An ATC works manually: the belayer has to physically hold the rope in the "brake position" to catch a falling climber. Holding the rope in the brake position bends the rope twice: over the lip of the ATC and under the carabiner. The two bends create the friction needed to prevent the rope from moving. You adjust friction in the system by changing how sharply the rope bends over the lip of the ATC. The sharper the bend (i.e. the deeper you move into brake position), the more friction there is.

A Grigri works automatically. When the rope "jerks" (i.e. the climber falls), the rope running against the internal cam reaches enough friction to move the cam so it pinches down hard on the brake end of the rope, thus keeping it from sliding. For the cam to engage, the friction between rope and cam has to be great enough. This is why new thin ropes with a slippery finish feed faster than thicker ropes, which have higher frictional properties due to surface area. The Grigri is equipped with a lever that disengages the cam, allowing you to pay out slack quickly and to lower climbers.

With the Grigri, you can feed out slack without depressing its lever by doing it *gently*—this is because the force is never great enough to match the frictional force needed to move the cam. In other words, the quicker the rope accelerates against the Grigri's internal cam, the better the Grigri locks down. A fall accelerates the rope, and the Grigri locks up nearly instantaneously. To feed out slack quickly, however, you must hold down the Grigri's lever so that the cam doesn't engage. There are various approved methods for performing this action safely. Learning how to feed out slack is vital to proper lead belaying with a Grigri.

If none of that makes sense, here's all you need to know: don't interfere with a Grigri's cam (or cam lever) in the event of a fall—the cam needs to move to lock down on the rope. Don't make a habit of keeping the cam lever depressed as some climbers mistakenly do in order to feed slack easier. Basically, let the Grigri do its job, and keep your brake hand on the rope.

TOP-ROPE BELAYING WITH AN ATC OR GRIGRI

Place your guide hand on the live end of the rope—about right in front of your chest.

Grab the brake end with your brake hand. When using a Grigri, a *thumb-away* position is more comfortable. When using an ATC, a *thumb-toward* position makes it easier to return to the vital brake position.

As the climber goes up, you will need to take in slack. You don't want to take in so much slack that you are tugging on your partner's harness; just enough so that you're "right there" with the climber.

Pull down on the rope with the guide hand while simultaneously pulling out and up with the brake hand. (See figure 8-4.) Eventually your brake hand ends up in front of your chest, even with your guide hand. Only work with a foot of slack at a time—pulling in too much may compromise your grasp of the rope.

Once you've taken in a foot of slack, you have to reposition your brake hand in order to take in another foot of slack. Remember: you're not supposed to take your brake hand off the rope, ever...so how do you slide your brake hand back to the device safely? Using your guide hand, pinch the

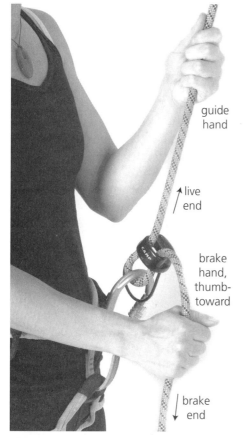

guide
hand

live
end

brake
hand,
thumb-
toward

brake
end

Fig. 8-3. Top-rope belaying with an ATC

Fig. 8-4. Taking in slack as the top-rope climber moves up the wall

brake end of the rope just above your brake hand to hold the cord in place. Now quickly *slide* your brake hand down the line until it is right back against the belay device. Never take the brake hand "off" the rope. You should end back at the first position.

In figure 8-5 the belayer has the brake end pinched with her guide hand and is sliding her brake hand down the rope toward the ATC. Notice she performs this entire sequence without taking her eyes off the climber.

Repeat these steps as the climber moves up the rock. Make small, incremental motions, constantly taking in slack. Anytime you're not taking in slack, return to the brake position: brake hand down, gripping the rope at the side of your hip.

How to catch a top-rope fall. With either an ATC or the Grigri, holding a fall is as simple as returning to the brake position: hold the brake end of the rope and sweep your brake hand down to the side of your body by your hip. (See figure 8-6.) You want this motion to become instinctive.

A Grigri, if used and loaded properly, will catch a climber by itself. Don't touch the Grigri device in the event of a fall—the cam has to engage for the rope to catch.

brake hand slides down

Fig. 8-5. Pinching the brake end with the guide hand allows you to safely reposition your brake hand.

Fig. 8-6. Brake position

Also, don't pull down on the live end with your guide hand, which may prevent the Grigri's cam from fully engaging. So take your guide hand off, keep your brake hand on, and let the device do its job.

How to lower with an ATC. When your partner reaches an anchor or wishes to come down, they will first call out, "Take!" Take in all the remaining slack in the system so that you feel your partner's weight. Then your partner will yell, "Lower!" or "Dirt me!"

Place both hands on the brake end of the rope in a *thumb-toward* position—your

elbows are slightly bent, not fully extended. Begin to let the rope slide through your palms while simultaneously adjusting the angle the rope runs over the lip of the ATC until you achieve a nice steady speed. Keep it smooth, and don't go too fast.

How to lower with a Grigri. With your brake hand on the rope, use your guide hand to pull the Grigri lever back slowly (figure 8-8), disengaging the cam. Don't yank it back all the way—keep it at 80 percent or so.

Now, soften your grip on the brake end of the rope so that it slides through your

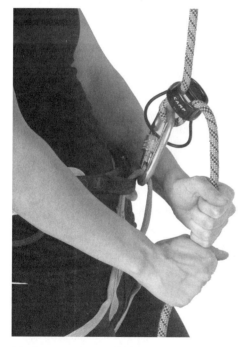

Fig. 8-7. Lowering a climber. Use two hands on rope.

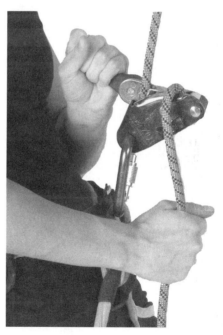

Fig. 8-8. Lowering a climber with a Grigri; guide hand pulls lever back and brake hand controls rope speed.

SOME CONSIDERATIONS WHEN LOWERING:

Kinks. As you lower your partner you will inevitably have to deal with kinks in the rope. Tight kinks can catch your brake hand off guard, compromising your grip and control of the brake end. Dealing with kinks is easier with a Grigri than an ATC because you can release the lever, locking the device down on the rope. Now you are free to shake out kinks. With an ATC, you will need to iron the rope kinks out with your guide hand.

Brushing. It's courteous to ask your partner if she wants to brush/tick any holds or practice any sequences on top rope. Hold her weight to allow her to do so.

Manage the rope's remaining length. It's your duty as a belayer to be conscious of how much rope is left as you lower your partner, so that your partner doesn't lower off the end of the rope. *Always* have a knot tied into the end of the rope.

Obstacles. On overhanging routes, when climbers are lowered out away from the wall, be conscious of trees. If there are trees, lower slowly as the climber works through them.

palm. It's friendlier on your hand to adjust the speed of your partner's descent with the Grigri lever as opposed to the pressure of your brake hand on the rope.

LEAD BELAYING WITH AN ATC

Lead belaying basically works the same as belaying a top-rope climber, only in reverse. Instead of taking in slack as the climber goes up, you will be paying out slack. Keeping your brake hand on the rope at all times remains critical.

Place your guide hand on the live end of the rope, and your brake hand on the brake end, *thumb-away.* This position makes feeding slack easier. Your hand position (thumb-away or thumb-toward) is ultimately a matter of personal preference—stick with what

feels best and master it. You want more slack in the system with lead belaying than with top-rope belaying. There shouldn't be so much slack out that the live end of the rope touches the ground, but enough slack to create a healthy bow or "dip" in the live end of the rope. This dip is important because it gives the leader the freedom to move, jump, clip, etc. without being hindered by a tight rope. In figure 8-9 the belayer has a healthy bow in the live end of the rope, and is also prepared to catch any fall with the brake hand safely holding the rope in brake position.

Feeding slack. Initiate by pulling slack out of the device with the guide hand. Simultaneously feed the brake end of the rope *into* the device with your brake hand. When your brake hand reaches the belay device, soften your brake-hand's grip and *slide* your brake hand down the rope, never

Fig. 8-9. *Lead belaying with an ATC*

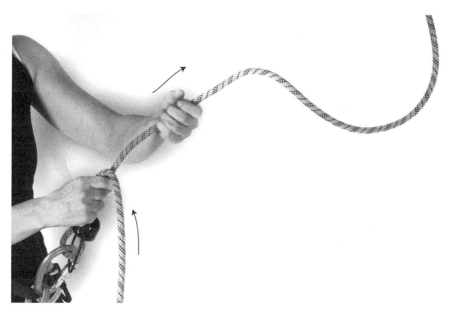

Fig. 8-10. *Paying out slack is a two-hand motion.*

taking it fully off. In figure 8-10 the belayer has pulled up slack with the brake hand while pulling it out with the guide hand.

Clipping. When a climber clips, feed slack as described above, only more rapidly. Raise your brake hand (with rope) up to stomach height and pull out hard with the guide hand, letting the rope slide through your brake hand. This can be a delicate maneuver because the timing is tricky. You don't want to feed rope too soon because if the leader falls without making the clip he will take a longer fall; however, when the leader grabs the rope to clip, he should not have to pull against a taut rope, which may sap his energy and send him off balance.

LEAD BELAYING WITH A GRIGRI

Lead belaying with a Grigri is similar to lead belaying with an ATC. Petzl recommends that you never take your brake hand off of the line. However, Petzl also admits that this is difficult to do and acknowledges that climbers must temporarily bend this rule when pinching down the Grigri cam/lever in order to quickly dispense slack. Whenever you are not feeding slack, *always* keep your brake hand on the brake end of the rope!

There are three basic positions/techniques for lead belaying with a Grigri: classic technique (thumb-away), new technique (thumb-toward), and lefty technique (upside down). These three techniques differ from each other only by how you

orient your hands to feed slack when the climber clips. Lefty technique also differs in how you clip the Grigri to your harness. Try out each technique to see what feels most natural. Ultimately you'll want to stick with just one to master it.

No matter which technique you use, make sure you don't switch the "role" of either hand. That means don't pull out slack with the brake hand—that's what the guide hand does; similarly, don't use your guide hand on the Grigri's lever when giving slack—that's a job for the brake hand.

Don't make a habit of keeping your hand on the Grigri; don't touch the device when catching a fall. Also, remember to properly load and lock the Grigri. Double-check the system, including the climber's knot and harness. Have the climber check your harness, locking carabiner, and Grigri.

CLASSIC TECHNIQUE

Position. Place your guide hand on the live end of the rope. Place your brake hand on the brake end in the *thumb-away* position (figure 8-11).

Feeding slack as the climber progresses. Feed rope into the Grigri with your brake hand while simultaneously and gently pulling slack out of the Grigri with your guide hand (figure 8-12). Pull too hard and the Grigri will lock up. It takes practice to get the feel of how hard you can pull out slack—and it's different with each rope.

Feeding slack when the climber clips. Slide your brake hand down the rope and *onto* the Grigri so that you are cupping the underside of it with your palm. With the

Fig. 8-11. Classic technique

Fig. 8-12. Feeding slack as the climber progresses

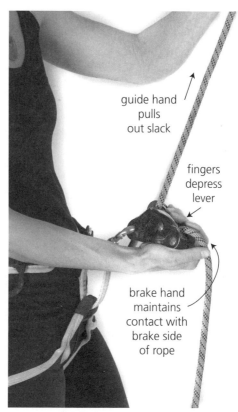

guide hand
pulls
out slack

fingers
depress
lever

brake hand
maintains
contact with
brake side
of rope

Fig. 8-13. Feeding slack when the climber clips

four fingers of your brake hand, depress the lever/cam and quickly pull slack out with your guide hand. (See figure 8-13.) When you've pulled out enough slack, quickly return your brake hand to the rope, thumb-away as shown in figure 8-11.

NEW TECHNIQUE

Position. Place your guide hand on the live end of the rope. Place your brake hand on the brake end in the *thumb-toward* position.

Feeding slack as the climber progresses. Feed rope into the Grigri with your brake hand while simultaneously and gently pulling slack out of the Grigri with your guide hand. Slide your brake hand back down the rope and repeat. This action is the same as the classic technique above only your brake hand is in the thumb-toward position (figure 8-14).

Feeding slack when the climber clips. Keeping the rope in the palm of your brake hand, position your brake hand on the Grigri so that your thumb reaches around the live end of the rope and depresses the fulcrum of the Grigri lever.

■ Use the pointer and middle fingers of your brake hand to steady the underside of the Grigri.

■ Hold the lever down with your thumb while simultaneously pulling up slack with your guide hand. Allow the rope to run freely against the palm of your brake hand (figure 8-15).

■ After the climber clips, return to your thumb-toward position on the rope as seen in figure 8-14. Make any

Fig. 8-14. New technique

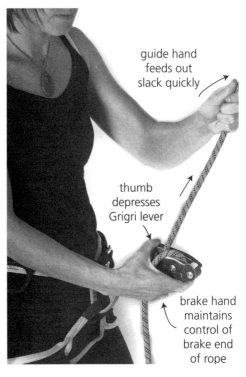

guide hand feeds out slack quickly

thumb depresses Grigri lever

brake hand maintains control of brake end of rope

Fig. 8-15. Feeding slack when the climber clips

adjustments to how much slack is in the system.

LEFTY TECHNIQUE

The Grigri and the techniques described above are designed to work best when the brake hand is your right hand, and the guide hand is your left. Lefties will prefer using their dominant hand as their brake hand, and they can do this by setting up the Grigri in a different orientation. The lefty technique described below allows your left hand to be the brake hand and your right hand to be the guide hand. Place your brake hand on the rope in the thumb-toward position.

Setup. Thread and load the Grigri as per normal, only clip it to your locking carabiner so that the Grigri is "upside-down." In this arrangement the bottom of the Grigri (with the Petzl logo) faces up at you and the rope faces away/toward the ground.

Feeding slack as the climber progresses. Use the brake hand to feed rope into the Grigri while gently pulling it out with the guide hand.

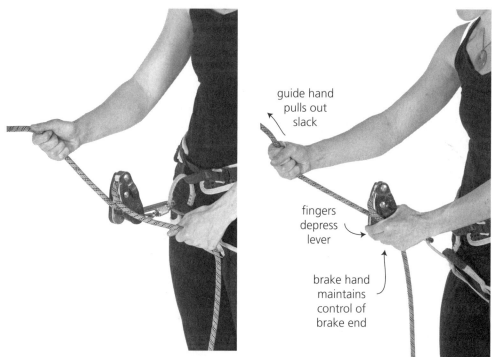

guide hand
pulls out
slack

fingers
depress
lever

brake hand
maintains
control of
brake end

Fig. 8-16. Lefty technique position: note the Grigri is "upside-down."

Fig. 8-17. Feeding slack when a climber clips

Feeding slack when the climber clips. With the rope in the palm of your brake hand, position your brake hand on the Grigri so that your pointer and middle fingers reach across the device and depress the fulcrum of the Grigri lever. Steady the Grigri with your thumb. Pull out slack with your guide hand. Allow the rope to run freely against the palm of your brake hand. (See figure 8-17.) After the climber clips, return to your thumb-toward position on the rope.

SITUATIONAL TECHNIQUES FOR GREAT LEAD BELAYING

There's more to belaying than simply mastering the hand motions needed to operate the rope and belay device. Herein lie the subtleties that will increase the safety of your belaying. Being a safe belayer will help your partner become a better climber.

THE BELAY BOX

Before a climber even starts up a route, inspect your surroundings—this is your "belay box." At some crags the belay box is small and confined due to trees and bushes, or even hazardous due to adjacent cliffs or drops. When there are others belaying nearby, the size of your belay box will be defined by the need to avoid their space.

The larger the belay box, the easier it is to be a great belayer. Once you see and define your belay box space, use it.

When the climber says, "Take!" one effi-

cient way to adjust the slack in the system— as opposed to taking in rope through the belay device—is to quickly backstep away from the wall. Scan your belay box first to spot troublesome rocks or tree branches that you might trip over. Clear packs, ropes, dogs, and gear out of the belay box before the climber even begins.

Likewise, if a climber says, "Clipping!" you can quickly give him a bit of slack by taking a quick step toward the wall while simultaneously paying out slack.

The point is that you should feel free to use the entire belay box to efficiently adjust the slack in the system.

Where to stand in the belay box. Knowing where to stand is an important part of giving a good catch. Most of the time you will want to post up close to the wall, beneath the first quickdraw. Standing out and away from the wall means that there's more rope out, which means the climber will fall farther than needed. Furthermore, if you're belaying out and away from the wall, and the climber takes a whipper, you will be pulled toward the wall and potentially slammed into it. I've seen some belayers, who were standing too far out from the wall, catch an unexpectedly big fall that literally knocked them off of their feet—the force of the falling climber dragging them across the ground until they slammed into the wall. Standing directly beneath the first quickdraw means that there's only one direction a fall could pull you: up, safely into the air.

Keep an athletic stance, one foot forward, the other back. Be prepared to jump, spring, move. Ask yourself, "What would happen to me if the leader fell right now? Would I slam into the wall in front of me?" Stay alert both mentally and physically.

Spotting. If the climber chooses not to stick clip the first quickdraw, stand directly behind the climber and give him a "spot" in case he falls before reaching the bolt. To spot a climber, get into an athletic stance and hold your hands up, aiming them at the climber's rear/waist area. If the climber comes off, soften his fall by *bumping* his rear or waist with your hands. You don't want to *push* a falling climber; rather, you want your arms to absorb a little impact. Try to prevent the climber from keeling over backward and hitting his head on the ground.

Passing the first quickdraw. After stick clipping the first bolt the climber may find it difficult to keep his legs from getting tangled in the rope if the route is steep. It's helpful to pin the live end of the rope close to the wall using your guide hand (keeping your brake hand on the brake end, of course). Once the climber's feet are even with or above the first quickdraw, resume normal belaying position.

How much slack? As the climber moves upward, follow him or her with a steady feed of line, keeping a healthy dip in the live end. Stay with and watch the climber. If the climber makes a big lunge up, you need to feed out rope at the same pace, keeping enough but not too much slack in the line so that the climber isn't restrained by a rope that's too tight. (See also "Giving a Soft Catch" later in this chapter.)

The constant adjustment. After clipping an overhead quickdraw, the climber will climb up to and past it. As a climber approaches the quickdraw, more slack develops in the system. Take it in. Always strive to maintain that healthy dip in the rope. Lead belaying is a constant adjustment of slack that assures just the right amount of it in the system.

Watching the climber/caring for your neck. Keep your eyes on the climber at all times. However, tilting your head back while your partner leads an entire pitch may make your neck sore. Take every opportunity to perform a two-second neck stretch. Press your chin to your neck and hold it there for two seconds, swaying your head gently back and forth.

On steeper climbs, it's better for your neck if you belay with your back to the wall, facing away from the cliff.

Taking. When a climber falls, or simply rests on the rope, the belayer holds his weight by taking in all the slack in the system and holding the rope with the brake hand in brake position. The quicker you take in all the slack, the better belayer you will be. Most of the time you spend belaying sport climbs will involve holding your hangdogging partner's weight. A Grigri will make this job significantly easier, but you can also do yourself a favor by sitting back in your harness and putting your weight on your heels.

When the climber yards up the rope. As a climber yards up the rope to regain a high point after a fall, he introduces slack into your end of the rope. Your job is to instantly absorb this slack while continuing to hold the climber's full weight.

Before the climber begins yarding, scan the belay box again for anything you might trip over. You'll be walking backwards away from the cliff, so choose the path you'll take. Now, with your weight on your heels as you face the wall, tell the climber it's okay to begin yarding up the rope.

A yarding climber should go slow, making one or two pulls up the rope at a time. Stay upright by keeping your weight on the heel of one foot; step the other foot behind you in preparation to weight it. As the climber yards, you will fall back onto this rear foot. Always stay prepared for this sudden introduction of slack. An unexpected yard up the rope has sent many belayers keeling over onto their rears. If a climber is yarding up the rope too fast, ask him to slow down.

Once the climber reaches the high point, he should go in direct. If he forgets, ask him to. After the climber goes in direct, walk back to your spot next to the cliff beneath the first quickdraw. Take in all of the remaining slack and wait for the climber's next command. He'll likely need to go "On you!" but maybe he wants to clip up, or call up the stick clip. Wait to see.

Jumping up the rope. If the belay box is small and there's not enough room to simply walk back while the climber yards up the rope, you can "jump up the rope."

Jumping up the rope means grabbing the live end of the rope with your guide hand and pulling down hard as you simultaneously hop up into the air and take in slack with the brake hand. (A Grigri is especially helpful here.) Done properly, you will end up a foot or so off the ground, hanging from the belay device on the rope. (See figures 8-18 and 8-19.)

Make jumping up the rope easier by timing your jumps with the climber's yarding. If you can pull down on the rope at the same moment that the climber yards up the rope, you'll have two forces working in your favor. Repeat as more slack is introduced.

How to belay a boinking climber. You have just caught a fall. If you're lighter than the climber, or you jumped up to give a soft catch, you should be hanging on the rope a few feet off of the ground. Don't lower yourself down to the ground just yet. Wait to see if the climber needs to yard up the rope or boink. A climber's yarding will automatically lower you to the ground.

To belay a boinking climber you want to remain hanging on the rope so that the full weight of your body is assisting the climber. Before giving the climber the go-ahead to boink, check beneath you. Is there a sharp tree branch or talus that could hurt you?

When the climber boinks, you will instantly drop between 6–12 inches. Simply allow yourself to drop until you regain your footing on the ground. Tell the climber to wait one second while you jump up the rope so you are once again fully hanging on the line. Continue this process until the climber can reach in and yard up.

Anchoring the belayer. There are times—though not many—when it is prudent to anchor a belayer to a tree, to the ground, to the wall, etc.

Some climbers mistakenly believe that it's safe climbing technique to anchor lightweight belayers so they don't fly into

Fig. 8-18. The belayer jumps up the rope to help a fallen climber yard up.

Fig. 8-19. The belayer jumps into the air as she simultaneously takes in slack with her brake hand.

the air when catching a fall. The concern is that a belayer flying into the air lengthens the distance of the climber's fall. However, as illogical as this seems, that's exactly what you want!

In general, anchoring your belayer is a bad call. You want your belayer to be free to move around in order to easily perform all of the above tasks—taking in slack quickly, jumping up the rope, and, above all, giving a soft catch. (See the next section.)

A hard catch accounts for the *majority* of injuries sustained from lead falls. Very few injuries occur because the belayer wasn't anchored.

If you weigh 100 pounds less than the leader, you may want to consider anchoring, but otherwise there's rarely any need. Exceptions include precarious belaying positions, such as next to a precipice or on a steep slab. Then, an anchor will prevent falling off a cliff. In these situations often the belay deck will have a fixed anchor available.

GIVING A SOFT CATCH

Aside from knowing how to safely operate the belay devices, giving a soft catch is the most important, and least understood, aspect of great belaying. Sport climbers rely on soft catches to not only keep them from

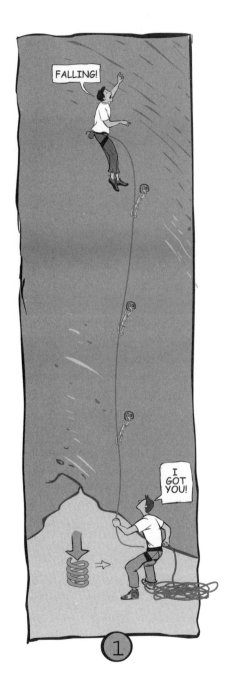

Fig. 8-20. Giving a soft catch is a matter of perfect timing. A soft hop in the air right as the falling climber passes the quickdraw will do the trick.

ROPE
GOES
TAUT

② ③

slamming into the wall, but to boost their confidence. Knowing that you'll get a safe, soft catch is the catalyst you'll need to begin pushing yourself on lead and expanding your free-climbing boundaries.

What a soft catch is and why it's misunderstood. The basic principle behind a soft catch involves introducing *more slack* into the system right at the moment the falling climber's weight comes onto the quickdraw.

Climbers have widely misconstrued this concept to mean that a soft catch is all about always having *more slack in the system*—meaning the belayer has a giant loop of slack out at all times.

Not true!

The amount of slack out prior to a fall is mostly irrelevant to whether a catch is hard or soft. More slack out prior to the fall simply means that the climber will fall farther—still possibly getting a hard catch.

Giving a soft catch means introducing slack into the system at the moment right when a climber's weight comes onto the quickdraw.

Imagine a pendulum: an object swinging back and forth on a rope. If you lengthen the rope halfway through the pendulum's swing, the object will slow down and not swing as far back and forth. Lengthening the rope *dampens* the speed and shortens the trajectory of the object.

A climbing fall is similar to a pendulum, only it's turned 90 degrees to vertical. There's the rope, the object (i.e. the climber), and the pendulum's fulcrum (i.e. the quickdraw).

The key to giving a soft catch is lengthening the rope right at the moment the climber swings onto the quickdraw. So, how do you lengthen the rope at the right time? Keep reading...but first, a story:

One of the most famous anecdotes of the soft catch in action took place at the base of the infamous runout trad climb *Rhapsody* (E11, or 5.14c R/X), in Scotland. Dave MacLeod, the bold Scotsman who did the first ascent of *Rhapsody*, made the common error of anchoring his belayer because he didn't want to fall any farther than he had to.

MacLeod fell off the final moves, well above his last piece of gear, dozens of times, and each time he took a 50–70-foot whipper. Because his belayer was anchored in, and therefore unable to give soft catches, MacLeod took hard swings into the wall. He sprained his ankles multiple times and bruised his body all over.

About two years later, Sonnie Trotter achieved the second ascent of *Rhapsody*. Like MacLeod he took multiple 50–70-foot falls. However, Trotter never once slammed into the wall. He never bruised his body and never sprained his ankles. In fact, Trotter said, "I actually thought falling was fun!" So, what did he do differently?

"Two things: slack and timing," Trotter said. The belayer remained unanchored, making it possible to "jump" up with the climber—something MacLeod's belayer was unable to do. This jump dampened Trotter's arc into the wall and made the falls softer. Trotter describes the timing essential to completing this task:

"Timing is crucial. Pay attention to the

leader. Have a small bow of rope in your hand, between the Grigri and the first quickdraw. When that bow comes tight, that's when you immediately jump and go with the momentum of the system. If you jump too early, you will come back down and get jolted and give the leader an even worse catch than if you had done nothing. If you jump too late, well, your leader will tell you what that feels like."

Perfect timing is essential to giving a soft catch. Wait to jump until you see the plummeting climber *about* to come even with the quickdraw he is falling onto. As soon as the rope begins to come taut, hop into the air. Giving the perfect soft catch is not a matter of *how high* you jump—just that you hop 6 inches into the air at the right moment. Your guide hand plays a crucial role in helping you with timing: When you feel the rope begin to move, hop.

If you're successful the climber will not slam into the wall but merely "kiss" it with his feet.

Heavier vs. lighter climbers. Giving a soft catch can be easy or difficult depending on how much you weigh compared to the climber. Lighter belayers will find that they don't always need to jump to give a soft catch. Heavier belayers have the hardest time of all. Giving a soft catch to someone who weighs 50 pounds less than you is quite difficult.

A lighter belayer who catches a big fall may need to worry about getting pulled into the first quickdraw. This is dangerous if the belay device gets stuck in the quickdraw's carabiner and causes the belayer to lose control of the rope. If this is a legitimate concern (e.g., the first draw is close to the ground and the belayer weighs 50 pounds less than the climber), the best solution is for the climber to not clip the first quickdraw. A climber can safely do this in one of two ways: Either stick clip the second quickdraw from the ground; or climb up to the second quickdraw, clip it, and then downclimb a couple of moves and unclip the first quickdraw.

Heavier belayers will need to perfect the timing of their jumps. Jumping too early or too late will likely result in a hard catch.

CHAPTER 9

Whitney Boland onsights the stunning Vesper (5.12b), Lime Kiln Canyon, Nevada. *(Photo © Keith Ladzinski)*

Onsighting: Strategies for Success

Though it happened way back in 1988, people haven't forgotten when the French climber Patrick Edlinger won the World Cup at Snowbird, Utah, the first international climbing competition ever held on U.S. soil.

A 100-foot vertical wall with a tiny roof in it near the top thwarted everyone in the field. Edlinger, one of the final competitors of the day, took his headphones off and walked up to the base of the wall without even looking up to inspect it. He tied in and very gracefully climbed to the top. Spectators there that day swear that when Edlinger pulled through the crux roof, the overcast skies parted and the evening sunlight cast a golden beam down upon the victor.

People remember Edlinger not just for succeeding where others had failed, but for the *style* of his ascent. It was the purity of his onsight—the fact that he walked up to the wall without looking at it, and climbed it so effortlessly and fluidly—that immortalized this moment in the annals of U.S. climbing history.

An onsight—successfully sending a route on your first try without any information (beta) about it—is the finest ascent you can make. In most cases you will only onsight climbs that are easy for you. Onsighting a hard route near your limit is probably the most difficult challenge there is in rock climbing. There's no shortage of things that can go awry—you can read sequences wrong, not see key holds, hesitate, get nervous, and pump out.

Onsighting is organic. When you do it, it feels like it simply just happened. Really, it's the culmination of all of the training you've done, the routes you've redpointed, and the things you've learned about reading rock climbs and executing moves efficiently.

Onsight climbing is perfection. It's the marriage of your strengths and experiences coming together to help you make an ascent in the best style possible.

ANATOMY OF AN ONSIGHT

Your onsight level is a function of your *physical* fitness and hardest recent redpoint, your *mental* readiness—your pre-climb motivation and state of mind, and your *experience*—your ability to read the route and execute moves efficiently. It is one part physical, one part mental, and a whole lot of experience.

Physical. Always try to onsight any route you get on that's below your hardest redpoint. You never know what will happen, so give it a shot.

The quickest way to improve your onsight level is to focus first on redpointing increasingly harder routes. Note that simply projecting a hard climb—working the moves, etc.—doesn't produce fitness (or confidence) until a successful redpoint.

Let's say your hardest onsight is 5.10d, and you've redpointed 5.11a in two tries. Your hardest redpoint ever is 5.11b. One of your goals this year is to comfortably onsight any 5.11a. Being able to onsight 5.11a sport routes would not only raise your standard as a sport climber but give you a lot more confidence and fitness for onsighting 5.10 trad routes, too.

This is a very realistic goal. However, even though you only want to bump up your onsight level by one grade, it may take up to a full year of weekend sport climbing to achieve it.

To reach this goal, you will want to work on redpointing *four* different 5.12a routes. Completing four different routes of a particular grade is the minimum standard for claiming a solid foundation at that level. Why 5.12a? Because the redpoint level for most climbers is four letter grades (i.e., one full number grade) higher than their onsight level. (Not coincidentally, this goes both ways: if you can onsight 5.12a, for example, you should be working on redpointing 5.13a.)

With four 5.12a routes under your belt, you will have gained the minimum fitness and experience you need to onsight just about any 5.11a sport climb.

Mental. Both redpointing and onsighting challenge the mind, but in different ways.

With redpointing, you know where the holds are and climbing the route is a matter of climbing well, having the fitness to link all the moves together, and overcoming any mental hurdles.

Onsight climbing is much more intimidating and uncomfortable because you don't know what's coming next—not to mention that you only get one chance to onsight a route. This may make you climb more statically and less fluidly. You may over-grip holds or be more hesitant to commit to the sequence. These errors result in an earlier onset of the pump and a lower likelihood of success.

How you deal with these hurdles depends on your temperament. Some climbers find that they onsight best when they have low expectations. For them the ideal state of mind is to stay relaxed and try their best without focusing on the outcome.

However, many climbers equate this detached attitude with giving up too early. On the ground, you'll hear them say, "Oh, I don't really care if I fall, whatever." Then, on the route they say, "Take!" at the first move that gives them a little bit of trouble or feels insecure. Onsighting isn't a gift—it's something you have to work for. It takes motivation and commitment to face the discomfort and intimidation of a new route. You have to *want it*.

Other climbers have the opposite problem. They become so consumed with *needing to onsight* a route that success takes on exaggerated proportions. They psyche themselves out—climb tense, get pumped quicker, and fall.

Where is the balance? How does one reconcile staying relaxed and unattached with a desire to succeed?

The first mistake is equating relaxation with indifference. Words matter. Don't say that you "don't care" about whether you fall or not. You should care!

However, it's equally important to have humility; after all, it's just rock climbing. The best advice here is a lesson from my uncle Suhail, who always told me, "Care...but don't care too much." It's simple but profound advice that I find relevant to just about every life situation, from work to world affairs to onsighting.

Before you get on a route, decide how hard you want to try. Do you want to onsight the climb? If you think it might be too hard to onsight, treat it as a redpoint project—hangdog your way up, figure out the moves, and give it the ol' One-Two (i.e., send it second try). However, if you are going to commit to the onsight, be resolute. Make a vow, *before you tie in to the rope*. It can be as simple as, "I am going to onsight this climb—it's going to be hard, but I will do my best." Simple, strong language. Believe in what you are saying.

After making that vow, don't psyche yourself out. You've made a mental commitment, so push it out of your consciousness for now. The commitment is irrelevant until you actually get on the route, so there's no need to dwell on it as you tie your shoes, tie in to the rope, and prepare to climb. Let any expectations float to the surface and evaporate like mist in the sun. Connect with your partner, joke around a little. Nothing will make you more at ease than a burst of laughter. As you tie in and boot up, think primarily about safety. Pay attention; be present.

Right before you get onto the route, take a deep breath, recalibrate your mind so that it's in climbing mode. Most important of all, *smile*. Now begin.

Experience. Onsighting is the art of free climbing. There is no shortcut to improving this skill—it comes only with experience. The more you climb and the longer you do it, the easier it becomes.

SENDING SIGHT-UNSEEN

Though nothing will substitute for years of getting out there and discovering what works for you, here are some real-world tips and beta to help you improve in this most protean style of ascent.

READING THE ROUTE

This involves being able to look at the rock, pick out the best-looking holds, and visualize how to climb them efficiently.

This begins on the ground. Look up at the climb and pick out as many features as you can. Look for white spots—which could indicate chalk marks (or it could indicate bird poop). The direction of the chalk often indicates the orientation of the grip. Try to see and imagine the left-hand/right-hand sequence for each hold.

When the sequence isn't obvious, look around for clues. Maybe you match on a lower hold, or have to cross through. Look left and right—is there an obvious feature you're missing? Maybe there's a hidden hold that won't reveal itself until you're on the climb. If you're still stumped, make a mental note of that particular section; remember to look around right before you reach it.

If there is no chalk, look for indentations, shadows, holes, pockets, and any other feature that might indicate a hold.

Also pay attention to the route's larger features. If the climb follows a corner, imagine yourself stemming up it. If the climb includes a bulging arête, look for heel hooks and oppositional holds that will help you hug the feature.

Most importantly, try to spot rests from the ground. Are there any obvious jugs? Resting jugs are typically coated in chalk due to climbers shaking out and chalking up (in fact, the more chalk there is, the bigger the hold tends to be). Is there any place to cop a stem and give your forearms a break? Spot any acute protrusions; maybe you can kneebar against it to rest or to help make a clip.

Deciphering an entire sport climb from the ground requires good spatial awareness and memory. It's a lot like seeing ahead in a game of chess. You have to anticipate every possible move and decide which one will work best.

After visualizing yourself climbing the sequence, it's time to execute. Just like in a chess game, you may have to adjust your strategy when the moves play out differently than anticipated. A good onsight climber is creative enough to change up his beta on the spot. Sometimes that requires downclimbing or matching on a hold. If you can't make these little adjustments calmly, collectedly, and without expending too much energy, it's checkmate (whipper).

MOVE FROM REST TO REST

Spotting rests from the ground will help you break the route down into "mini-routes"— the sections between each rest. Think of rests as "checkpoints" you must reach, one at a time. Focus on moving steadily and efficiently from one resting place to the next.

If the rest is great, stay there until you're back to 100 percent. While resting, look ahead and gather as much information about the upcoming sequence as you can. If the sequence is hard to decipher, it will make leaving the rest more committing. What if you screw up? Don't let this fear psyche you out. Success or failure is irrelevant if you give it your best shot.

Sometimes rests aren't as good as we hope. Maybe the hold we thought from the ground was a jug ends up being a sloper. Knowing how long to rest in these situations takes a keen awareness of your own body and its ability to recover.

Ethan Pringle, who has onsighted 5.14a, says that resting too long is a mistake he sees many climbers make.

"I think a good rule of thumb is don't rest longer than the time it took you to reach the rest," he explains. "It took me a long time to realize this. For years, I would shake out forever because I could hang on forever, but then I would get to a long move and I would be spent."

In other words, if it took you 60 seconds to climb up to the first rest on the route, don't rest longer than 60 seconds.

BE EFFICIENT

Efficiency of movement is at the core of great free-climbing technique. Being efficient on the rock means not wasting energy or adding extraneous foot or hand moves. Efficiency is fluidity. It means getting a rhythm going and achieving a feeling of *flowing up the climb.*

Learning to be efficient is best done in the gym, where all the holds are marked and there is usually only one sequence (as opposed to real rock, which often offers multiple sequences). Spend a lot of time climbing easy routes in the gym, flowing up the holds to an internal rhythm. Top roping teaches this flow as well. Efficiency does not necessarily mean climbing faster. It means moving to a beat and not stuttering.

The ability to read rock quickly and move over it effortlessly comes with experience. Broaden your experience by visiting new areas and climbing on as many different types of rock (or plastic) as you can.

BE DECISIVE

Many onsight attempts fail when a climber's indecision or hesitation meets a difficult sequence or when the forearms get a little pumped. The climbers who succeed more often than not are those whose brains work faster. How can you get yourself out of this mess? Come up with a plan in a split second and commit to it. Be decisive and execute. Sometimes that means simply relaxing more.

HAVE PATIENCE

Being decisive, however, doesn't mean rushing the move. As important as it is to be spontaneous, it's equally important to have patience while you climb.

Fig. 9-1. Visualize yourself climbing up the wall: the body positions you'll need, where the rests are, and eventually standing on top. (Photo © Keith Ladzinski)

Fig. 9-2. Lauren Lee displays patience and poise in a most exciting position—high up in the Verdon Gorge, France, on the classic route Eve Line *(5.12c).* (Photo © Keith Ladzinski)

One of the more common errors we commit is rushing to reach the top. Climbing can often feel uncomfortable or even scary. Our natural instinct is to rush to the top to end the discomfort as soon as possible.

Part of climbing, and especially onsighting, is learning how to respond to the discomfort—mental and physical—of the route. Don't rush. Make the next move when it feels right. Make sure your feet are properly set, and that you are in balance to move. Maybe you will need to place a foot higher, even if that foothold is worse, in order to be balanced.

Identify the problem and have the patience to solve it. If the next handhold seems out of reach, look for a higher foothold. Have you missed any handholds—an undercling, perhaps, that will allow you to make the span? Again, don't rush the move.

Stay in the present. Focus on making only one move at a time—and make it perfectly. This applies to both onsighting and redpointing.

TRY SOMETHING DRASTIC

Alex Honnold, who has onsighted 5.13b sport routes and 5.13d trad routes, says that some of his hardest onsights are the result of just going for it. "Being able to commit quickly is key," he says. "Rather than spending time and energy worrying if you're doing it right, just do it one way or the other. I've onsighted several routes where I made blind dynos or throws around bulges because I just assumed there had to be a hold there. I'd get to a point where I was stuck, and figured there was only one place I couldn't see, and therefore there had to be a hold there. Then, I'd go for it. Of course, I've fallen like that too, but that's life!"

FLASHING

The best way to improve your onsight level is to work on flashing routes that are hard for you. Flashing trains the part of your brain that must be decisive but patient; and it teaches you how to climb unfamiliar moves efficiently on your first try. You will still need to read the rock when flashing a climb, but not to the degree you would during an onsight.

What is good beta? The single difference between onsighting and flashing is having beta. Getting good beta beforehand is crucial to flashing a hard climb, while bad beta usually leads to a fall. If you're choosing to flash, as opposed to onsight, a climb, there's no reason not to get as much beta as you can. Once you know one thing—such as the location of a hidden hold in the crux sequence—you may as well find out *everything*: Is there a redpoint crux? Where are the rests? Are there any tricks to resting in those places (e.g., a kneebar or heel hook, etc.)? Are there any difficult clips, and what hold do you clip from? Are there any clips that you want to skip?

Getting beta involves asking other climbers who have done the route before. The people who have the best beta for a route are the ones who have spent time projecting the route. Even people who have not yet redpointed the climb may have excellent beta. Also, good beta is dependent on body size. A five-foot-one-inch climber probably won't want to ask a six-foot-five-inch climber for beta. The shorter climber could learn a few things from the taller climber, but the beta should be taken with a grain of salt.

If you get the chance to watch a climber do the route first, even better. Study the body positions and remember which ones look unobvious, such as a high heel hook or a wide stem.

Finally, if the person with the beta is standing at the base of the route, feel free to ask him or her for tips while you are actually climbing. If you are the person giving the beta, it's helpful to be as descriptive as possible. Give simple, short directions and use creative, descriptive names to describe the holds. "High-step your right foot on the tooth, and grab the basketball sloper with your left hand!"

THE ELEMENTS OF STYLE

Onsighting has become a lost style of sport climbing as climbers focus on ticking the next higher grade through redpoint tactics. Even in the media, reports of hard onsights have fallen by the wayside due to the higher numbers generated by hard redpoints.

There are some admittedly nebulous rules about what constitutes an onsight. Indeed, over time the word has been used with increasing carelessness. Climbers say they have *onsighted* something when in fact they have actually *flashed* it—not to be dishonest but because they don't understand the difference between the terms. Imagine if someone said he had aced a test when in fact he had received the answers from a friend.

By the strictest definition, an onsight means free climbing a route—successfully and on your first try—under the following three conditions:

1) You place your draws during the ascent (no preclipping).
2) There is little or no chalk and few, if any, tickmarks indicating where the holds are.

3) Aside from knowing the grade of the climb and its name, you don't know anything about the route—not where the crux is or what the style of difficulty is like (powerful, dynamic, endurance, etc.). Not knowing the grade of the climb adds to the purity of an onsight.

These conditions have softened with time, partly due to logistical reasons. At many crags it is impossible to onsight purely due to preexisting chalk, tickmarks, and quickdraws. So, it's now currently acceptable to claim an onsight even if there are fixed quickdraws and the route has chalk marks. The most important thing is that you don't know anything about how to perform the crux sequence, or where it is on the route.

OTHER QUALIFIERS THAT WILL INVALIDATE AN ONSIGHT

Stick clipping. Stick clipping the first bolt is okay, but creating a mini–top rope by stick clipping two or three bolts up the route not only takes away from the onsight but might invalidate the ascent (especially, say, if the route is only four or five bolts long).

Downclimbing to the ground. If you climb up to the first bolt, clip it, and downclimb to the ground, you still have a shot at onsighting the route as long as you don't rest too long. However, some climbers take this concept too far: they climb up a route, clip bolts, and then downclimb to the ground after advancing the rope up the climb. Some go as far as resting for an hour (or even a day), and then climbing up the first half of the route with the benefit of knowing where the holds are and the mini–top rope. This style invalidates an onsight.

Getting beta midroute. Another way to invalidate an onsight is if your friends on the ground tell you what to do, especially where holds are: "There's a jug just left!" They can even ruin it for you by shouting something quasi-specific such as, "You're almost there!" As vague as that seems, knowing you're "almost there" is akin to knowing that the difficulties are about to relent. Cheers such as "Good job!" and "Kill it!" are fine.

Watching someone else go first. Watching someone else on a route tells you a lot of information: where it's hard, where there are rests, and so on. Thus, if your partner goes first, and you have to belay him, you won't be able to claim an onsight on your turn. Sorry. If the onsight is that important to you, ask if you can go first, or find someone else to belay your partner.

Using binoculars. Some sport climbers from Europe—where onsighting is a bigger deal than here in the United States—use binoculars to study the holds from the ground. This won't invalidate an ascent, but it is a little strange.

TRY CLIMBING WITHOUT A GUIDEBOOK

Aside from flashing routes, one useful strategy for improving your onsighting is to go to a new area or crag without a guidebook. Pick routes based on how good and how hard they look *to you*. It's amazing how knowing the difficulty of a route beforehand will change your perception of it. There have been plenty of times when I've looked up at a climb and thought, "That doesn't look too bad," only to find that the guidebook gives it a harder rating than I would've guessed. The climb then becomes more intimidating, which changes the confidence I bring to the route.

Leaving the guidebook at home will also help you with your rock-reading skills. You'll naturally study a climb more intensely if you are trying to determine if it is doable. It's also a good exercise in self-reliance and judgment: two key components to the outdoor rock-climbing experience. Don't get on anything you think could get you in trouble. Take precautions. Rely on your safe ropework skills and great belayer to get you up and down the route without injury.

That said, don't be afraid to go for it! While passing through Maple Canyon, a sport climbing area in central Utah, Chris Sharma picked two routes that he simply thought looked like good fun—and onsighted them both. Only later he learned that the routes were both 5.14b, and were the two hardest climbs at the crag.

Ignorance can be bliss—without a guidebook you may shock yourself when you take down a hard route on your first try.

CHAPTER 10

The master of redpointing, Dave Graham fires an incredible 5.13c at Tres Points, Spain.
(Photo © Keith Ladzinski)

Redpointing: Techniques for Sending

With your quickdraws up on your route of choice, it's time to begin the often frustrating, occasionally enjoyable, and eventually rewarding process known as projecting the route.

In terms of style, projecting is the heart and soul of sport climbing. Hangdogging, beta rehearsal, preplacing gear and tickmarks, ruthlessly wiring cruxes—these are some of the classic tactics that climbers employ to redpoint a route at their physical and mental limit. The modern techniques and strategies in this chapter will help you go even further.

The term "redpoint" dates back to the early 1970s in Frankenjura, Germany's largest climbing area. Here, the local climber Kurt Albert drew a small circle at the base of a climb that had not yet been completed. When the route was finally sent—that is, free climbed from the bottom to the top without falls—Albert filled the circle with red paint. The German word *rotpunkt* (rot = red, punkt = point) birthed the term redpoint.

A redpoint differs from an onsight or flash in that a climber takes more than one attempt to free climb a route. Originally, one qualifier of a redpoint ascent had the climber placing draws or gear as they ascended—climbing a route with preplaced draws or gear was disparagingly called a "pinkpoint." This distinction, however, is now all but obsolete.

THE RIGHT TEMPERAMENT

The redpoint style of climbing is not for everyone. Working on a route for days, weeks, or sometimes years takes a particularly determined personality. Do you like adversity? What about monotonous adversity? Imagine climbing on the same old rock holds, day after day, only to fall at the same spot, again and again.

For some people, the projecting mentality comes naturally; I was not one of these people. It took me about two years to appreciate the redpoint style of climbing. I hated falling on moves that other people found easy. I hated projecting other climbers' warm-ups (I still do). I hated the tedium of climbing on the same route every day. It felt like work when climbing is supposed to be anything but.

More than anything, I hated the tremendous pressure I placed on myself to redpoint. Once I knew it was possible to succeed, I felt an anxious dagger carving me up inside, a feeling absent when climbing easier routes onsight. I felt obligated to redpoint, like it was something I *had* to do. I especially hated it when this anxiety caused me to tense up and fall again.

But I kept at it because I believed (and still believe) that projecting makes you a better climber. It really does. Not only that, but the process of working a route can reveal certain strengths and weaknesses that you don't see elsewhere. Eventually this becomes the point of the rather pointless exercise called sport climbing. Stick with it, even when it sucks, and take comfort in knowing that climbing becomes difficult for everyone at some level. That's what we're here for. There's nothing to be learned from the easy path. The point is finding

your limit and then pushing it. If working a route feels like *work*, that's because it is. But nobody ever died from a little hard work, so let's get into the tactics that will help you combat the colossal forces impeding the long journey to a successful redpoint.

ALWAYS LEARN AND MAKE PROGRESS

Learn something each time you climb a route, and you will make progress with every attempt. Ingrain this advice into your projecting mentality, and you will not only find yourself doing harder routes in fewer tries, but you will be a smarter climber.

If routes were books, one might say climbers tend to skim. The righteous path is to study, then practice, and finally master the information at hand. To send a hard route you have to learn it. You want to be able to visualize every single hold within a few trips up the route. Eventually you'll know these holds better than your family, and you'll love/hate them just the same.

Find a slightly better hand position, discover a new rest, or use a higher foothold (even if it's worse) to do a reachy crux. Constantly reevaluate your strategy and don't hesitate to change it. Maybe you rest longer at one spot, or maybe you don't rest at all. Experiment. Don't climb with blinders on. The name of the game is to *find the absolutely most efficient way to move upward*.

Learning on a route isn't exclusive to the free-climbing beta either. You could spend your projecting session learning how to clip a hard-to-clip quickdraw better—finding a more efficient body position or learning to cross-clip instead of matching on a handhold. You could learn that a big fall is totally safe, and as a result feel more relaxed and willing to go for it the next time you're in the runout zone.

The great upshot of this most general advice is that learning gives you purpose even on days when you're not feeling strong. You can always learn something new, even on off days. If you feel weak, like there's no chance of redpointing that day—don't worry. Go up on your project anyway. Use the off day as an opportunity to hang on every bolt and to study your project better. The point isn't necessarily to be climbing better with each burn, but to be mindful of the learning process, which shouldn't end for any route until it has been redpointed.

BREAK IT DOWN

Difficult routes always seem intimidating and unfathomable at first, like the famous 72-ounce steak challenge at the Big Texan restaurant, in Amarillo, Texas. Your only hope is to cut it up and take one bite at a time. If a Texan can take down half a cow, you can send 5.12, 5.13, or even 5.14. Why not?

First, break the route down mentally— logically and elegantly. When you look at your project and no longer see a 100-foot nightmare but rather a managcable stack of three to five sections (a good range to shoot for), you will have created the building

blocks of the strategy you'll use to send the route.

All climbs can be deconstructed. Often, routes break down by physical attributes: where the cruxes and rests are. For example, let's say a 100-foot route has a pumpy start leading to a definitive crux followed by a good rest and capped by a "redpoint crux" before the anchor. In this example, there are four to five distinct sections: the pumpy start, the crux, the rest, and the final run (which can be broken down into two sections if the redpoint crux is problematic). Regard each section as its own mini-route, and work on sending each section independently.

Some routes, however, are sustained the whole way, and cutting them down becomes trickier. An obvious divider is the number of bolts. If there are five bolts, then there are only five sections you have to do. Use creativity to help yourself digest each piece. Tell yourself, "If I can do five boulder problems in a row in the gym, I can do this route."

A bad way to break a route down is to divide it by where you fall, since that point may change from day to day. Also, breaking the route down by where you fall is a typical mental error that creates a self-fulfilling prophecy. The rock presents enough challenges without negative thinking.

EARLY ATTEMPTS

On initial tries you will likely be hanging on every draw. Also, expect the first time up a new project to possibly end your day, and definitely crush you like a pumped little insect. That's normal so don't be blue. Stay positive, and use the opportunity to learn. Experiment with beta, extend draws for easier clipping, place thumbprint-sized tickmarks where needed, and memorize subtleties of holds and body positions.

Climb to the next draw and clip it. Always try to successfully complete the clip before saying "Take!" Grabbing quickdraws is a bad habit to get into: the more accustomed we are to grabbing quickdraws, the harder it becomes to not grab them.

That said, don't be afraid to grab quickdraws every now and then. It will always be safer to snatch a draw than take a whipper with slack out. If you pull up the rope, but feel yourself about to fall, just drop the rope and quickly grab the quickdraw by its dogbone. A nice beefy nylon dogbone is easier to hold than the lightweight 10mm Spectra ones.

In one infamous effort to make a desperate clip on *Hand Me the Canteen Boy* (5.12d), in Rifle, Colorado, Tony Yao lost his right pinkie finger. The rope trapped his fifth finger against the carabiner's basket just as he fell, and under his plummeting weight the rope came taut. His digit popped off his hand like a crab leg at a Cajun restaurant. Fortunately, Yao still cruises hard 5.13s despite having one three-pronged paw straight out of *The Simpsons*.

There's no shame in grabbing draws; it's better to be safe than to take a bad fall. But conditioning yourself to grab draws is just one more hurdle that you're eventually going to have to face in order to redpoint. Squash the habit early on and focus on the climbing. Force yourself to make clips and after doing so, always try to make one more move, no matter how flamed you are. You won't fall very far and this will train you to climb *through* the clip.

TECHNIQUE

Skip it or clip it? If one clip is giving you trouble, consider skipping it. The crux of a sport climb should be the free climbing, not clipping the rope to a quickdraw.

Judging the safety of skipping a clip demands experience. Usually, any bolt high up an overhanging route is okay to skip because the worst that can happen is you'll fall further through the air. As long as you don't hit anything, a fall through the air—even a big one—is safe. Skipping a clip that's close to the ground is obviously more dangerous because you run the risk of decking. Err on the side of safety.

If you decide to skip a clip, consider extending the next quickdraw so you can clip it sooner. Or consider using a shorter quickdraw on the bolt below the skipped clip in order to shorten any fall you may take.

Extending quickdraws. The *wrong* way to extend quickdraws is to simply chain two draws together, carabiner to carabiner. This is a bad idea because it rotates the bottom quickdraw 90 degrees, increasing the chance that you will backclip and the rope will unclip itself in a fall. Here's the right way to extend a quickdraw:

1) Go in direct to the top carabiner.
2) Take the bottom carabiner off the quick-draw.
3) Now take a secondary quickdraw and clip the top carabiner to the webbing of the first quickdraw.

Never clip your rope through the center carabiner of an extended quickdraw because it will cause the rope to run against

Fig. 10-1. The proper way to lengthen a quick-draw

the nylon of the lower dogbone. Only run your rope through metal!

Shortening quickdraws. There is no way to shorten a quickdraw other than using a shorter quickdraw. It's technically okay to clip a rope to a single carabiner on a bolt as long as the carabiner doesn't lie flat against the rock, but this is not ideal because it makes clipping hard. It's always better to use a quickdraw. Don't chain two carabiners together.

GOING IN DIRECT

When you fall or take, go in direct to your high point. Once you are safely hanging from the bolt, the belayer pays out a length of slack, enjoys a free moment to move, stretch the neck, and become reestablished at the belay. Likewise, use this time to compose yourself, relax, and breathe. Review what you have just climbed. Look at the holds. Learn them.

Common knowledge says that most people must see something three times before they learn it. Keep that in mind. Experiment. Try something ridiculous—maybe a dyno would be less pumpy! You have nothing to lose. Find the most efficient way to climb from bolt to bolt.

Ask yourself, "Why did I just fall?" Was it from being pumped? Were you grabbing the holds too tightly? Or were you off balance? Study the holds and visualize a different body position.

Now is also a good time to place tick-marks on hard-to-see hand- or footholds.

Take a chalk pebble and make a thumbprint-sized mark above, to the side, or below the hold. Brush chalk off of handholds, too.

When you feel rested, call down, "Take!" to your belayer. Once the belayer has your weight, unclip the dogging draw and place it back on your gear loop.

Always lower down three moves before getting back on the wall. You always want to practice climbing *into* the next sequence.

MAKING LINKS

Climbers often project a route by climbing until they fall, resting for a random bit of time, trying again, getting a couple of holds higher, falling again, and repeating. One day they either reach the anchors or give up and admonish themselves for not having enough strength and endurance. This behavior is like banging your head on a wall to get into a new room instead of using the door.

After you've mentally broken a route down into sections, it's time to start linking them together. Understanding how to make links is at the core of redpointing. The strategy you use to make links will not only be different with every route, but the process will become more innate and intelligent with experience. Still, there are some basics.

The most important rule. Spend most of your time wiring the top half of the route. This important link is the one that climbers most often dismiss. They spend a disproportionate amount of time working out the crux, writing off the run to the anchors as something they'd never fall on.

BEATING THE Z-CLIP . . . BY Z-CLIPPING?

As mentioned in chapter 5, Z-clipping is incorrectly clipping a higher quickdraw by pulling up slack from beneath a lower quickdraw. A Z-clip is bad because it causes the rope to run like a Z through two quickdraws, which will prevent you from getting even one move higher.

Z-clipping happens only when there are two quickdraws close together. To prevent Z-clipping, a climber pulls up rope from his knot. When the lower quickdraw is at your waist, you will need to pull the rope up three or four times to create the slack needed to clip the higher quickdraw. This can be really annoying, not to mention inefficient—you have to hang from one arm for longer than on a normal clip, which is taxing.

In these situations, one nifty trick I learned from the 5.14 climber Emily Harrington is to intentionally Z-clip the rope. Reach down, and pull up slack from below the lower quickdraw and clip it to the higher one. That's right, Z-clip on purpose! Now, to undo the Z-clip, simply unclip the lower quickdraw from the rope and—*shazam*—you're no longer Z-clipped.

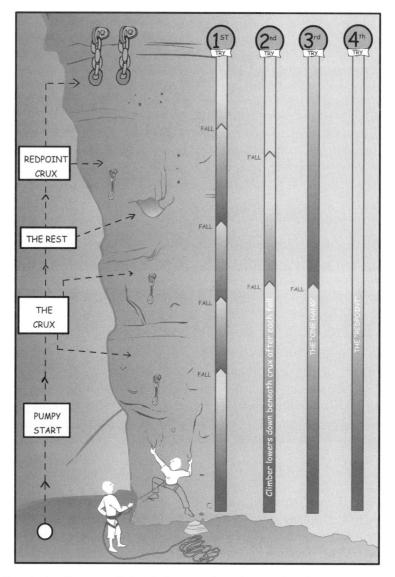

Fig. 10-2. To redpoint, first mentally break the route down into sections then work on linking the sections together: overlap continuous free-climbing movement through each section and into the next one in order to put a route together.

Problem is, *they haven't accounted for how pumped and tired they will be* after doing the lower moves in succession—they reach the so-called easier climbing, forget where the holds are, and fall.

You will make it through the crux one day. When you do, you want to be sure you'll send.

Link wherever else you can. Make links wherever and as often as possible. The purpose of making links is to train your brain to think in unifying terms. You are putting the route together. The basic idea is to first wire each section, then to link them, eventually climbing the route with three hangs, then two. Next, you want to achieve the pivotal One Hang.

Unfortunately, making links means fighting hard even when you're not on redpoint. This can be mentally difficult to do. If you've already fallen, why not just grab a draw or rest on every bolt? Avoid this easy path. You must fight to make links with the same tenacity that you will eventually use in fighting to redpoint the route. Often the former feels more taxing than the latter because the route is still new and the moves unfamiliar. So what? As the Spanish say, *Venga la muerte!* Climb to the death!

When projecting a route, always go to the top. Don't be lazy. When you are working on making links, always go to the top of the route. Even if you are too tired to link the upper part of the route, and have to hang on each bolt, don't even think about lowering off the climb until you are at the anchors! This accomplishes multiple goals: it pushes you out of your comfort zone; it's

good training; it's an opportunity to learn the moves and memorize the holds. And it will make you a better climber.

"WORK" THE RESTS

Sport climbing is often more about learning how to rest than it is about pulling hard moves. As you project your route and work on making links, learn the rests with the same dedication you learn the crux sequences. If you're lucky, your project has a rest where you can recharge your battery to 100 percent.

As you begin to push yourself on harder routes, the rests become more mental than physical reprieves. Even with straightforward rests, there are complexities that aren't necessarily intuitive. Learning to shake out on a still-pumpy hold, for example: you may not fully recover, and the longer you stay there the more fatigued you become.

In this situation, the goal isn't to rest your forearms but to slow your heart rate. Focusing on relaxing your heart rate—instead of your forearms—brings composure and a clear head to the very uncomfortable situation of hanging from the wall with pumped, aching muscles. With a clear head and a relaxed demeanor, you can climb through the fatigue.

Remember to hang from your skeleton. Use the friction between your skin and the rock. Use minimal strength to grip the holds, as little as you can while still remaining on the wall. Scan your body: where does it feel tense? As Lynn Hill counsels, "With a single exhalation, you can bring relaxation anywhere." The absolute best training for this technique is yoga. I highly recommend taking an Iyengar yoga class once a week. It will teach you how to breathe, meditate, and find repose in physically taxing poses.

HIGHS AND LOWS

As you start giving your project serious burns, always strive to reach a new high point—i.e., the highest point you can reach from the ground without falling. If you're lucky, it'll be the top!

If you fall, however, work on gaining a new low point, i.e. the lowest point on a route from which you start and can climb without falling to the anchors. This is also called working a route "top down."

The basic idea behind top-down projecting is that you can send from the last bolt to the chains, then from the penultimate bolt, and so on. Eventually, you will link the first bolt to the top, and if you can do that you can send the route.

Top-down projecting is more theoretical than practical. No one follows this bolt-by-bolt succession so strictly, nor should they. It is wiser to act reasonably and try to overlap the route's sections as it makes sense. Find a point in the middle of one previous section and overlap from there to the top of the subsequent section.

Joe Kinder, one of America's top sport climbers, says, "You must make links starting before the fall spot, even if it is three moves before. Gain confidence: it is the key to climbing hard!"

Top-down projecting is especially useful when a route is a sustained, power-endurance pump fest. With this kind of route, redpointing from a succession of lower bolts makes more sense. You will not only dial in the most important part of the

ROUTE RELAXATION SEQUENCE

- Upon reaching a rest, immediately focus on your heartbeat. Listen to it.
- Flex your abs while you relax your forearms, then vice versa. Let your face muscles melt. Smile.
- Slow and lengthen your breaths. Take deep three- to five-second breaths, but exhale normally.
- Drop your shoulders: in fact, do it right now. It's surprising how much tension this simple motion can release.
- The slower and deeper you breathe, the faster your heart rate will drop. Learn to individually relax every muscle in your body (including your heart) with a single breath.

climb (the top), you will also gain the fitness needed to do it. Gaining fitness for sustained routes can take a long time, so don't get discouraged. Top-down projecting is the best training there is for gaining the specific endurance needed to send the route.

The logistics of working a route top down can be confusing, but I suggest this: if you fall, always try for the One Hang. If you fall again, go to the top anyway.

Let's say you fell at the crux, which is at the fifth bolt. You got back on, fell again at the eighth bolt (the redpoint crux), and then went to the top.

Now that you're at the anchors, don't just lower to the ground. This is your time to climb, and since your muscles are warm and you are able to access any point on your project, take advantage. Choose a point on the route that you will lower down to and attempt to send from there. In this case, starting just above the crux and making it through the redpoint crux to the top will be a good confidence booster because you will have proven to yourself that it is possible to climb every move in succession above the crux. When you make it through the crux one day, you want that confidence that you can definitely do the rest of the route.

Pick a link you think you will nail. Since you've already failed to send, and failed to One Hang, make a new goal for yourself—one that you can achieve. Maybe, instead of lowering all the way down to just above the crux, you only lower to just below the redpoint crux, and climb from there to the top. The goal now is to feel like you are making progress.

Pulling the rope midroute to reload the top half of the climb. Lower down from the anchor to the bolt you want to start from. Use your dogging draw to tram into the line, hopping it under each quickdraw you pass. Once you reach the low point, go in direct.

You have two options. The simplest one is to top-rope back up. This is the best, safest, and most common method you'll use. Top-roping up the top half of your project is a good chance to work on your free climbing. Focus on pace. Feel comfortable on the moves, and *flow* up them.

However, maybe you fell at the redpoint crux because you've been having trouble clipping a bolt. Or maybe you grabbed the draw because you were afraid to take the fall. In other words, maybe something other than the free-climbing movement is giving you trouble. Simply top-roping back up the route won't address these issues. If that's the case, a better way to work the route from the low point is to pull the rope through the anchors and reload to the top.

What follows is a safe way to clip into one bolt and untie your knot to pull through the anchor, all while remaining on belay:

1) Starting at the anchor, tram into the rope with your dogging draw and lower down to the bolt you want to start from.

2) Go in direct. Pull up a bight of rope from the belayer's side of the rope and tie a figure eight on a bight. (See figure 10-3.) Clip this knot into a small locking biner, and clip the locker to your belay loop. The belayer keeps you on belay. If the

in direct

figure eight on
a bight clipped
to harness with
a locking biner

main
knot

*Fig. 10-3. After having gone to the anchors, the climber has lowered to below the redpoint crux. He
will untie and relead the top half of the route in order to work this important link.*

the anchor

redpoint
crux

main
knot
untied

Fig. 10-4. The climber is in direct to a bolt and tied to the rope (still on belay) with a figure eight on a bight.

Fig. 10-5. Retying into the rope end after having pulled the rope through the anchors

Fig. 10-6. Having retied in, the climber unties the figure eight on a bight. The belayer takes in all the excess slack until he once again has the climber's weight.

bolt you are hanging from pulls, you have the security of a backup knot and the belay.

3) It's now safe to untie your main knot and pull it through the anchors (figure 10-4). Make sure you completely undo the knot before pulling the rope down.

4) Pull the rope completely through the anchors and tie back in to the rope end (figure 10-5). Double-check your knot.

5) Untie the figure eight on a bight. The belayer quickly pulls in all of the slack and takes your weight (figure 10-6). When you feel your weight being held by the belayer once again, unclip your draw tether. Now go to the top!

THE ONE HANG

Ah, the all-important One Hang! Nothing signifies that a climber is ready to send a project like the One Hang. Climbing your project with just one fall is to redpointing what wooing a crush is to the first kiss. You've bought flowers, gone on the requisite two dates, and met the parents. Conditions are prime for smooching, and you just need to make sure you don't say anything stupid. And by that I mean you don't fall at the top of the route.

However, don't go patting yourself on the back just yet. A One Hang does not make, or guarantee, a send. I know climbers who have climbed their project with a single hang over twenty times before finally giving up.

Still, the One Hang is the best indicator that you are close to sending, and once you do achieve a One Hang, it's time to go into battle mode: get a good night's sleep before your day out, eat and hydrate well, and warm up properly.

Troubleshooting the One Hang. Here are a couple of uncommon solutions to common redpoint errors.

More rest: You are likely not waiting long enough in between burns—almost no one does. On endurance projects, wait at least one hour, and as long as two hours, before trying the route again. Eat snacks and drink water. Consider ingesting small doses of caffeine. While resting, don't make the common mistake of just sitting around. Research has shown that "active recovery" decreases the amount of time it takes to recharge your energy reserves. Doing light exercise speeds your body's processing of the lactic acid in your forearms and back. After any taxing burn on a project, take an easy 20-minute hike. Even doing a lap on an easy climb will help you recover quicker. Massage your forearms vigorously.

Break through: Perpetual one hangers have trained themselves to fall at the same spot. This mental block has caused more falls in sport climbing than cruxes have. Making a breakthrough often requires changing your perception of the route somehow. Try climbing on an even harder route for a while and coming back to your project—maybe it won't seem so bad.

Change something: Another great trick for beating the one-move trouble spot is to change something. Find new beta, even if it's harder. Yes, that's right. Do a different

10-7. Emily Harrington enjoys the steep, friendly jugs of the Motherlode, one of the best walls at the Red River Gorge, Kentucky (Photo © Keith Ladzinski)

sequence. Break the mold. New beta will get you out of the rut you're in.

WARMING UP FOR THE REDPOINT

"Not warming up properly is the biggest error I see climbers make," says Jon Cardwell, the preternatural climber from New Mexico who crushes 5.14d routes.

Indeed, properly warming up is the least understood and most beneficial thing climbers can do to help put them in a zone of top physical and mental performance.

Cardwell says he tries to do 100 moves before attempting to send an endurance route. Routes that are 80 feet long have 25–40 moves on them. Three to four routes of increasing difficulty is usually a good warm-up. The final warm-up should climax with a grade roughly one full number grade below your project. If you are projecting a 5.12b, try doing a 5.10a first, then a 5.10d, and finally a 5.11b.

What are you warming up for? Is your project short and powerful? If so, try warming up on an easier but still powerful route (as opposed to an endurance route). Another option is to climb a regular warm-up using a different style: instead of climbing slow and steady, make quick, powerful pulls between holds to awaken those fast-twitch muscles.

Consider what your project's crimping is like. Small, crimpy edges require more warming up. If your project has some small holds, don't warm up on jugs only. Consider making one of your warm-ups an onsight. Trying a route that you've never done before awakens your mental muscle in a way that climbing the same old warm-ups does not.

The basic idea is to get pumped but not be taxed. You want your forearms to be swollen but not shot for the day. After warming up, rest at least thirty minutes before getting on your project. Stretch, drink water, relax, and visualize yourself redpointing. Get psyched to try hard.

MORE TIPS FOR REDPOINTING SUCCESS

Only make one move at a time. Often we become so focused on doing an upcoming crux that we screw up earlier sections.

Never treat a route lightly. Lynn Hill once offered me this counsel: "Stay in the present. You only have to make one move at a time. So make each one well." How perfectly can you execute each and every move, even the easy ones?

Find a mantra. When Tiger Woods was a child, his father gave him this mantra to think about as he was sinking putts: "My will is strong. I do it all with my heart. I focus and give it my all." A good mantra will focus you before getting on a route, or even as you shake out at a resting hold and prepare for an upcoming redpoint crux. A good mantra sharpens your focus, gives you confidence, and psyches you up.

My mantra goes: "Don't overgrip, place your feet, climb strong, be confident." My mantra addresses my weaknesses (bad footwork and overgripping), and reminds me to focus on avoiding those weaknesses by being strong and confident in my abilities. I say this to myself before redpoint attempts and sometimes at rests.

Rock out. If your head is seriously giving you trouble and changing the beta doesn't work, put some headphones on and climb with an iPod. The music works to simultaneously distract and relax you. You might forget to fall where you usually fall because your favorite song is on. (Keep in mind that climbing with music may interfere with communication and safety.)

Pay attention to your pacing. Tommy Caldwell says the most important thing he thinks about is the pace of his climbing. He strives to find a tempo that allows him to climb smoothly and efficiently. "I start climbing faster and faster as I work the route," says Caldwell. "Finding that balance of climbing fast but being relaxed is tricky. You want to be as efficient as possible, but keep the heart rate low." On difficult, especially bouldery, cruxes, flowing through the moves becomes more important. A great way to work on pace is on top rope.

Battling nervousness. Feeling nervous before a redpoint is common. Turn this negative feeling into something positive. If you are feeling nervous, take that as a good sign: it means your mind thinks you are ready to send!

The B.S. Burn. This warms you up like a microwave: instantaneously. Climb up to the third (or so) bolt, come down, rest for five minutes, and begin for real. This tactic is especially useful when it is cold out: climb until your fingers are sufficiently cold, then come down and let them thaw out. As soon as they feel warm, start climbing. Your fingers are less likely to go numb.

***Always* try hard!** One of the most frustrating attributes I see in many sport climbers is how easily they give up. If they accidentally screw up some beta—perhaps the order of their foot sequence goes slightly awry—they freak out and say, "Take!" This happens even when they are on redpoint!

If you're on redpoint and you're still on the rock, *don't take.* You never know what could happen. Be a warrior and battle through any errors. If you're still on the rock, you still have a chance to redpoint. Compose yourself when you make an error, try to fix it, and continue climbing. Let the fire and passion of climbing burn inside you.

CHAPTER 11

Jen Vennon zeroes in on one of the country's best 5.13a routes, *Joe Six Pack, Virgin River Gorge, Arizona.* (Photo © Keith Ladzinski)

A Day at the Crags

The premise of this book is that climbers can take their existing levels of fitness and climb much harder by sport climbing more. Knowing how to approach a route at your limit, project it, and eventually redpoint it will get you further in climbing than doing pull-ups and lifting weights. That's not to say that climbers shouldn't train, because that helps, too. But many climbers don't know how to take their existing fitness and efficiently utilize it to their benefit in the outdoor climbing arena. They mistakenly equate failure outdoors with physical weakness, and while sometimes that might

be the case it's often true that the solution involves a smarter, better strategy.

Thus far this book has shown the rope-work techniques and redpoint tactics one needs to go up and get down. It has also given many mental and physical tips for becoming a better free climber. And it has shown how even having a great belayer, and being one yourself, will indirectly translate to being a better free climber. But these concepts are only useful if you know how to incorporate them into your day at the crag.

How you use the information in this

book—that is, how you spend your day at the crag—makes a difference. Each day at the crag is a blessing: we get to go outside and be away from our computers, push ourselves in an exciting medium, and revel in the sheer frivolity of climbing rocks. But each day out is also important to the grand scheme of becoming a better free climber. There's opportunity to improve every day if we're smart about it. Here are some real-world tips to think about as you take the concepts in this book to the sport crag.

WARM-UPS

The first thing you want to do upon getting to the crag is warm up. Doing this properly will be the most important part of your entire day.

Climbing two routes is the minimum warm-up, and three routes is even better. A good first warm-up won't make you flash-pumped (that sudden introduction of lactic acid into muscles that aren't yet warm causing pain and cramping). A second warm-up should be a little harder, but not much. You are still wakening your body to the stresses of climbing a vertical wall—don't rush the process. The third warm-up route should make you pumped. It should be hard enough that you need to work to send it, but not so hard that you're going to fall all over it.

Your warm-ups can be routes you've done before, but doing a new route is always more taxing than running a lap on something you know well.

At your home crag, you will want to work on expanding your warm-up options by repeating as many moderate routes as you can as often as you can. The better you know a route, the easier it will be to warm up on it. When you're on a climbing trip to a new area, it's a good idea to warm up by sampling many of the crag's moderate routes.

CRAG ETIQUETTE: THE QUEUE AND WORKING THE WARM-UP

At sport climbing areas, warm-ups often breed conflict between climbers of different abilities. A good five-star route may be a warm-up for an advanced climber but a project for an intermediate climber—thus making it doubly popular.

The advanced climbers sometimes try to cut ahead by saying something like, "Oh, this is just a warm-up for me. I'll be done quickly." Even if that's true, statements like that make intermediate climbers feel *worse*, which simply isn't cool.

The proper way to queue up for a rock climb is to walk up to a party at the base of the route and politely ask if anyone is going next. Find the order and place your rope bag down as a placeholder for your turn.

On the other hand, intermediate climbers should also be aware that projecting the crag warm-up may be considered irritating. A better bet is to simply wait an hour, when the route may be free and it will be okay to hangdog on it for as long as you need.

WHAT KIND OF DAY IS IT GOING TO BE?

This is a good question to answer before you even get to the crag—maybe even the night before. There are at least five "types" of days sport climbers can have, and each may require different mental or physical preparation.

Visiting a new area/pumping laps. When you get to visit a new area, or only have an afternoon at any crag, just go climbing and enjoy it. Don't worry about redpointing, onsighting, success, or failure. But just because the day is carefree doesn't mean you can't take every opportunity you can to try to improve latent weaknesses. Treat each route you get on as an opportunity to practice climbing perfection. Expand your comfort zone at least once: try to onsight a hard route, or take a whipper, or see if you can successfully send a full pitch at the end of the day when you are tired and will likely fall. Push yourself a bit, but mostly just have fun.

Going project shopping. When you decide you want to find a hard route to work on—something that will take you between ten and twenty attempts—you get to spend a day or two "project shopping." These days are fun but also taxing. Any time you go up a hard route for the first time, expect to get *worked*. Project shopping days are fun because there's no pressure to succeed; you just get to sample a new route and enjoy the thrill of figuring out the sequences. After getting to the top, ask yourself if you like it. You want to find a route you enjoy, something that motivates you, because you're going to be spending a lot of time on it. You're not looking for a one-night stand, but a route that you can have a meaningful relationship with...but only for a while because the relationship ends as soon as you redpoint.

Work days. Many days will likely be allocated to working on redpointing your one big project. This will involve warming up, giving your project one or two burns, and then "warming down." Work days can be extremely unmotivating and potentially depressing. The key to making work days enjoyable is to find happiness in the small steps you achieve. If you've learned a new sequence, or found a new hold, or made some good links, take it as a sign that you're making progress. Always find ways to encourage yourself.

Consider doing more warm-up climbs before getting on your ultimate project. When, as a teenager, Chris Sharma was working on *Necessary Evil* (5.14c) at the Virgin River Gorge, he steadily ticked off just about every other route at the area in between his burns on what was once the country's hardest route.

Try doing four pitches before getting on your main project: make the first three warm-up routes you've done before. Make the fourth one a moderately hard route that might take you only two or three tries to redpoint. (Not two or three tries on that day, but rather two or three days, with one attempt on each day.) Then, after that fourth pitch, get on your main project. This is not only a good way to tick new climbs, but you will continue building fitness. Further, quickly redpointing subsidiary routes will keep you motivated to climb.

Performance days. After you've achieved a One Hang on your main project, plan on having a performance day the next time you're out at the crag. On performance days, don't get on any hard subsidiary routes. Only do three, or even just two, warm-up routes before giving your project a burn.

If you send, congratulations! You can spend the rest of your day project shopping... or drinking beer and heckling your friends. If you don't, try to send the subsidiary project. And if you don't send that either, then you will have had a pretty standard "performance day" for sport climbing!

Fitness days. It's a good idea to take a break from work and performance days every now and then. Even if you haven't sent your project, take a day off from working on it when you begin to lose motivation, spending the day building fitness instead.

Fitness days involve getting in as many pitches as you can. Just go out and climb. Don't even think about your project. Take a day to just go climbing: spend it trying to onsight new routes or run laps on routes you've already done. Enjoy climbing routes you can do without falling. Incorporate more fitness days into your routine. For every three work days you put in, add one fitness day.

Always make a fitness day the *second* day. In other words, make Saturday a performance or work day, and make Sunday a fitness day—not the other way around.

WARMING DOWN

Consider spending the second half of your day working on a "secondary project" to warm down.

Climbers often migrate around a crag depending on what the sun is doing—either chasing the sun's rays, or more often avoiding them so they are climbing in the shade where it's cool. A secondary project could be a hard route that gets afternoon shade/sun.

Having more than two projects at once is not recommended. Projects demand a lot of attention and motivation, and it's too difficult to bring that energy to more than two routes at a time.

After giving your secondary project a burn or two, you will likely be too tired to do anything else, but you should force yourself to do one or two more pitches to warm down. Your secondary project should be two or three grades easier than your primary one.

If you spend too much time projecting a route—e.g. hangdogging at every bolt without making any links—it's possible to lose the fitness needed to climb for an entire rope length. Climbers counter this potential

Fig. 11-1. Shopping around for a new project is always fun. Here, Lauren Lee experiences the fun movement of Sharma Project (5.13d), Hurricave, Utah. (Photo © Keith Ladzinski)

fitness loss by warming down. Just as it's important to have a good, reliable warm-up routine, it's equally valuable to have one or two routes you can run a lap on at the end of the day. These routes should be fairly hard—there should be a 10 percent chance that you'll fall before reaching the anchor. Dig deep and summon the motivation needed to send these warm-down routes at the end of the day.

HOW TO CHOOSE A PROJECT

What is your hardest onsight? What is your hardest redpoint? How many routes of that grade have you redpointed?

The answers to these questions will help you choose a project. Typically you will want to work on redpointing routes that are one full number grade (or four letter grades) harder than your hardest onsight. If you've onsighted 5.11a, then 5.12a to 5.12b is a good range to shoot for.

The best way to progress through the grades is to systematically redpoint more routes below your hardest redpoint. You need to build a large base before attempting to stack a bigger block on the structure. The more 5.11d routes you've redpointed, the easier it will be to redpoint 5.12a. The more 5.11c routes you've onsighted, the easier it will be to onsight a 5.11d.

It's a good idea to redpoint a minimum of four routes of a particular grade before shifting up to the next level. Redpoint four 5.12a routes before getting on a 5.12b.

Also, consider what style you are good at. If it's bouldering, consider trying to redpoint a short, powerful route that fits your strengths. That said, to become a great climber, you must test yourself by redpointing routes that don't match your strengths. Thus, when working on achieving those four routes of a certain grade, make two of them routes that will test your weaknesses. So, two short and bouldery 5.12a routes, and two long and sustained 5.12a routes will give you a solid base to move on to a 5.12b.

The first time you attempt to redpoint a new grade is always the hardest. Successfully sending your first 5.12a or first 5.13a will be much harder than sending your second one. Part of this is physical, but 90 percent of it is mental. Breaking into a new grade requires that you battle the uncertainty that you're capable of doing a route of that difficulty. Don't restrict yourself by tying your brain into knots. Let your belief in your abilities be expansive and open to the idea of success.

Conversely, some climbers mistakenly think that climbing one 5.13a will automatically make others come much easier. It's not uncommon, however, to put in just as much work for your second, third, and fourth. Maybe by the time you've redpointed fifteen of them, they will begin to feel easier.

MOTIVATION

Inspiration is permanent, motivation is temporary. You could be a truly passionate climber by nature but still have days when you're just not motivated to climb. Motivation, however, is arguably the most important determinant in our climbing performance. Sport climbers tend to be obsessive, proud, and pig-headed. They have a hard time admitting defeat when there is a serious motivation-vacuum. If you feel unmotivated to climb, have enough love and respect for yourself to say, "It's okay if I don't go climbing today, or this week, or even this month." Motivation is like hunger—it's an empty feeling that craves satiation, whether that means a big meal or a lot of pitches. We will not be motivated if we become glutted on climbing, just like we are not hungry after we eat a big meal. It's healthy to fast from climbing, because, like a pang of hunger, the desire always returns.

Finally, there's no shortage of dumb

things that motivate people, from their own ego, to not wanting to "suck," to money. But how often do you allow yourself to be motivated by other people who you care about and vice versa?

Surrounding yourself with positive people is the one surefire way to keep the motivation high. Climbing with people who are better than you makes you better, *rapidly*. It can be difficult to find happiness in seeing another person succeed, but opening yourself to the possibility of this symbiotic happiness taps into a deep and plentiful wellspring of motivation and inspiration.

CRAG ETHICS

Access to sport climbing areas is not guaranteed. Each of us needs to be a responsible, ethical member of the climbing community if we hope to climb in the places we cherish. Please pay attention to the following guidelines.

- **Don't litter.** Pack your trash in and out. Don't leave garbage behind, even if it's not yours.
- **Poopy ethics.** Don't poop near the cliff, and don't piss where the rain won't wash it away. If you need to go number two, go 100 yards away from the cliff, dig an eight-inch hole in the ground, poop there, and fill the hole back up. Pack out toilet paper, or burn it. In some high-use or environmentally sensitive areas, it is better to use a wag bag.
- **Dogs.** Dogs are only well behaved according to their owners. Well, that's not always true, but the point is that Fido is inevitably less cute and adorable to other people than he is to you. Always bring bags to pack out dog poop. Teach your dog not to walk or sit on ropes and rope bags. Apologize profusely if your dog misbehaves. Keep your dog on a leash. Best of all, don't bring your dog to the cliff at all.
- **Don't make trails.** Stay on established paths, and don't blaze shortcuts through vegetation without a landowner's permission.
- **Don't alter the rock.** Never, ever chip or alter the rock. It's bad enough that we place chalk on the walls (scrub it off when you can).
- **Replace bad gear.** Even if the gear is not yours, replace worn slings/quickdraws and old/sharp carabiners, especially on the anchors. If a route needs new bolts, ask an experienced bolter to replace them—and chip in to buy new hardware. Keeping an area safe and accident-free will help keep access open.
- **Speak up.** If you see a climber doing something unsafe or dumb, let him know. Be bold and confident, but also polite. Sometimes people are simply ignorant and will appreciate the safety tip.
- **Don't place bolts on traditional climbs.** There is more than enough rock for everyone to be happy. Please don't bolt lines that can be traditionally protected. At the same time, trad climbers should be open to allowing good-looking, unprotected face climbs to be bolted even in traditional-climbing

areas. Ultimately, we are all climbers. Regardless of what type of protection we clip, there are more similarities than differences between us. Find common ground and mutual respect for each other, and be reverent and thankful for how varied and diverse climbing is.

■ **Be friendly.** Say hi to non-climbers and be nice. Don't shout curse words when you fall. Be a good ambassador for the sport. Don't bother coming to the crag unless you're there to have fun.

Jen Vennon samples the granite of Red Faction (5.13a), Crystal River Valley, Colorado.

Where to Go: The Best Sport-Climbing Areas and Crags

There are hundreds of great sport-climbing spots around the country, but here are a few of the best, presented in alphabetical order.

There are many online resources that can direct you to your nearby local crags, but a good place to start is by asking the owners of your local gym where to go. But traveling to go climbing is one of the sport's greatest gifts, so if you get a chance, plan a trip to visit some of these excellent destinations.

MAPLE CANYON, UTAH

Located in central Utah, the conglomerate cobbles of Maple Canyon offer some of the most unusual and interesting rock climbs in the United States. Large, rounded river pebbles welded in a sandstone matrix on a gently overhanging wall make the climbing here fun, engaging, and a good place to gain endurance.

Routes range from 5.4 to 5.14, and the grades seem to vary wildly between different walls. You may find that you can on-sight 5.12 at one wall, and yet not be able to do the first move of a 5.12 at another wall. The walls are between a 10- and 50-minute hike from the high-altitude campground.

The cobbles can be solid, but they can also break easily in some places. Bring and wear a helmet, especially if you are belaying. Don't sit beneath climbers either.

Techniques to learn here: Hanging effortlessly from the sloping cobbles on overhanging walls is the name of the game. Sometimes pockets are hidden behind the cobbles themselves. Learn to be creative and use the cobbles efficiently. Learn to do crazy toe hooks, heel hooks, and kneebars here. Onsight climbing can be tricky, but that said, if you happen to grab the right cobbles on your first try, you might think Maple is a great place to onsight.

Where: Approximately two hours south of Salt Lake City, near Ephraim.

When: The best temps in Maple Canyon are between the spring and fall. Summers can be hot but the low humidity, altitude, and shade make it a good time of year to visit.

Other Utah sport crags: American Fork, Causey, Mill Creek, Uintas Mountains, and the dozens of crags around St. George.

NEW RIVER GORGE, WEST VIRGINIA

Located deep in the heart of West Virginia, the New River Gorge was once known as the crack-climbing capital of the East Coast and is now renowned for its hundreds of five-star sandstone sport climbs.

The diamond-hard rock of the New is carved by one of the oldest rivers in North America. Between the New River Gorge proper, Summersville Lake, and the Meadows, there are now at least 1600 established routes on over 60 miles of cliff line. The best grades are in the 5.10 to 5.13 range, with a few 5.14s thrown in for good measure. Some of the routes may require additional trad gear to supplement the bolts.

Many walls are approached from above, and hikes can take 15–45 minutes.

Techniques to learn here: Aside from being a great place to try your hand at crack climbing, the New River Gorge offers overhangs, roofs, faces, and dihedrals that present many opportunities to learn classic free-climbing body positions. The sport climbs have distinct cruxes between easier climbing and good rests. This is also an excellent area to hone your face-climbing skills.

Where: The New is just outside of Fayetteville, voted one of the top ten best climbing towns by *Rock and Ice* magazine. There is also excellent kayaking and mountain biking in this scenic wilderness area.

When: Fall is best. Spring is good, but often wet. Summersville Lake is a great summer crag because it is shady and situated beside its namesake lake. With climbing options on both sides of the river, you can stay in the sun or shade depending on the season.

OBED, TENNESSEE

The high-friction, bullet-hard sandstone cliffs rising out of the convergence of the Obed River and Clear Creek are some of the best in the Southeast. You'll find over 400 routes here, most in the 5.7 to 5.12 range, with some routes as hard as 5.14. Huge horizontal roofs and jugs characterize the features of the Obed—crags look tiered like the underside of a staircase.

Many of the climbs are as short as 40 feet, but some routes are longer than 100 feet. You'll never have to hike more than 30 minutes to reach the climbing, and some routes are only two minutes from the car. Make sure you bring a stick clip, because many first bolts are high off the ground.

Techniques to learn here: The roofs that define the Obed are great for learning the core strength and awareness needed to climb steep terrain. Also, you'll learn how to mantel to pull over the lip of a roof. With many changes in angle over the course of a single pitch, the climbing is as fun as it is mentally and physically demanding.

Where: The Obed is 45 minutes northwest of Knoxville, near the town of Lancing.

When: Fall and spring are best. Several south-facing walls make winter climbing an option. Summer is hot and humid.

OWENS RIVER GORGE, CALIFORNIA

California's biggest sport-climbing area is the Owens River Gorge, located just outside of Bishop. The volcanic tuff of the Owens River Gorge presents five-star vertical routes in the 5.10 to 5.11 range, many of them 100 feet long. There is not much steep climbing here, but there is some. You will need a full 60-meter rope to get up and down the many 100-foot routes.

The Central Gorge is decked-out nicely, and it's possible to pump laps all day on 5.8s, 5.9s, and 5.10s.

Techniques to learn here: The long vertical walls of the Owens River Gorge offer opportunities to perfect your economy of movement, find efficient sequences, and learn to rest on good holds. It's a great place to gain endurance and get into climbing shape.

Where: The climbing is in the high desert foothills of the stunning Sierra Nevada Mountains. The climbing is only 20 minutes outside of Bishop, an awesome base for all

breeds of vertical adventurers. Also near Bishop is the world-class bouldering of the Buttermilks and the clean, granite alpine peaks of the Sierras.

When: The canyon runs north/south so there is always a wall in the sun and one in the shade. Climbing is best in the fall and spring, but year-round climbing is possible.

Other California sport crags: Echo Cliffs, Malibu Creek State Park, New Jack City, Holcomb Valley Pinnacles, El Cajon Mountain, Jailhouse, Donner Pass, Clark Mountain, and many others.

RED RIVER GORGE, KENTUCKY

The Red, as it's affectionately called, is one of the largest and best climbing areas in the country. Since the mid 1990s, route development at the Red has taken off as entire new walls and crags are found annually. There are over 2000 routes at the Red—half of them are sport climbs; the other half are trad climbs, making this Kentucky region a multidiscipline climbing paradise.

The Red is also distinguished for its number of five-star routes of all grades, especially in the 5.8 to 5.14 range.

The rock is conglomerate sandstone that forms huecos, pockets, crimpers, and slopers. Some cliffs are short, but most are long (some as high as 250 feet). The Red is renowned for huge jugs on steep, overhanging rock.

The Red River Gorge has a tight-knit climbing community formed from a geographically diverse region. Every weekend, hundreds of climbers from all over the Northeast, Midwest, and Southeast descend upon the Red and stay at Miguel's Pizza, a family-run restaurant, gear store, and campground.

Techniques to learn here: Routes are long and pumpy. With large, skin-friendly holds, the Red is a place to gain endurance and learn the technique of hanging on with as little energy as possible.

Where: The Red River Gorge is located 45 minutes outside of Lexington, Kentucky. The hub of activity is Miguel's Pizza, a good base for reaching the many spread-out crags. A 4WD is helpful for reaching many of the crags.

When: October and November are crisp and beautiful, and early to late spring can be great, but rainy. Summers are muggy and hot, while winters can be brutally cold. Many people climb here year-round.

RED ROCK CANYON, NEVADA

This massive climbing destination has it all: bouldering, multipitch trad and sport climbs, and a great collection of user-friendly single-pitch sport climbs that come into prime condition during the winter months when everywhere else is too cold. Plus, Red Rock is just 20 minutes outside of Las Vegas, which, depending on what you are into, may or may not be a good thing.

The sandstone here is soft and climbing is not recommended within 24 hours of rainfall. Fortunately Red Rock is in the desert and this is rarely an issue.

Red Rock has something for everyone. You'll find over 150 climbs in the 5.12 to 5.13 range, and an equal number of climbs under 5.9. There are close to 500 routes in everyone's favorite range: 5.10 to 5.11.

Techniques to learn here: The climbing here is crimpy, so learning to trust small edges will be a priority. That can be hard to do, however, because the rock is brittle and may break under your weight. The rock can be sharp, so bring your skin and pain tolerance. Routes vary from short and bouldery to long and technical. Some of the country's best multipitch sport climbs reside here, such as the six-pitch *Prince of Darkness* (5.10c).

Where: Twenty miles from the Las Vegas Strip.

When: The sport climbing in Red Rocks is best in the winter, from November to March.

Other sport crags near Las Vegas: Mount Charleston, Potosi, Arrow Canyon, Virgin River Gorge, Lime Kiln Canyon, and Clark Mountain.

RIFLE MOUNTAIN PARK, COLORADO

Rifle, a beautiful box canyon with a babbling creek running through it, is the best limestone sport-climbing area in Colorado. While there are fewer than 300 routes here, most of them are 5.12 and harder. In fact, a general rule here is that the harder the route is, the better it is. There are more 5.13d routes in Rifle than any other grade.

There are some great moderate routes here, too, but this is mostly a crag for experienced free climbers. The climbing is unique because you rarely pull *down* on holds. Instead, routes are climbed using awkward body position on blocky features.

Ben Rueck enjoys the cool breeze of Western Slope stone, Colorado.

The footholds are notoriously bad and polished.

No approach takes longer than a few minutes, and in some places you can actually belay sitting on the hood of your car.

Techniques to learn here: This is the place to go to learn what it means to project a route. Due to the bizarre blocky features, onsighting here is extremely difficult. Most routes also require kneebarring to do cruxes—as opposed to other areas where kneebars are merely used for rests. Bring kneepads and prepare to be humbled. Also, due to its abundance of slippery, polished footholds, Rifle is a great place to learn how to really stand on bad holds.

Where: Just 15 minutes outside the cowboy town of Rifle.

When: Spring and fall are good, but Rifle is best during the hottest months of the summer. The canyon runs north-south, meaning there's always a wall in the shade.

Other Colorado sport crags: Penitente, Clear Creek Canyon, the Monastery, Flatirons, Independence Pass, and the Frying Pan crags on the Western Slope.

RUMNEY, NEW HAMPSHIRE

Rumney offers hundreds of high-quality sport climbs of all grades, from 5.3 to 5.15a, on a unique rock type. The granite schist of Rumney is very grainy—in some places it looks like petrified wood. Due to the granite grains, the friction is high, but it can be also be pretty sharp.

The climbs are located on a maze of cliffs tucked away in the forest. Rumney's twenty-three rock outcrops have distinct flavors, which keeps the climbing varied and interesting. None of the cliffs take longer than 30 minutes to walk to, and it's pretty standard to visit three or more cliffs per day.

The easy and moderate routes are well bolted and perfect for learning to lead. At many of the walls it's also possible to lead easier climbs and set up top ropes on adjacent climbs. The crags with the best beginner routes are the Parking Lot Wall, Darth Vader, Main Cliff, Jimmy Cliff, and the Meadows.

Techniques to learn here: Routes are short and the climbing tends to be powerful. Rumney is a wonderful place to gain power-endurance and pure strength. Boulderers will love Rumney for its hard cruxes, while gym climbers and beginners will love the plethora of 40-foot introductions to sport climbing.

Where: Rumney Rocks is located on Rattlesnake Mountain, just outside of the quaint college town of Plymouth, in central New Hampshire.

When: The best time to visit is the fall. Spring can be wet; summer is hot and swarming with black flies; winter is generally too cold and snowy.

Other Northeast sport crags: Shagg Crag, Maine; Sundown Ledge, New Hampshire; Bolton-area crags, Vermont.

SHELF ROAD, COLORADO

One of the earliest sport crags in the country also happens to be one of its best. Located outside of Colorado Springs, Shelf Road is a beautiful, peaceful climbing area in the desert. This is a premier area to learn how to sport climb.

Shelf Road has over 500 limestone routes, most in the 5.9 to 5.11 range. Just about all of the routes are well bolted, and the climbing is straightforward and easy to read. There are also some great 5.12s and 5.13s, such as Colorado's first 5.13a, *The Example.*

Techniques to learn here: With technical, vertical face climbing of all shapes and sizes, Shelf Road has it all. The routes tend to involve using pockets, crimps, and jugs on arêtes, through roofs, and up dihedrals. This is a great place to pump laps and get a good workout.

Where: The walls of Shelf Road are found in the Royal Gorge, just outside the sunny city of Cañon City, 45 minutes south of Colorado Springs.

When: With great, stable weather, almost any day is prime from the fall to the spring.

SMITH ROCK, OREGON

Smith Rock is known as the birthplace of American sport climbing, even though the area originally was (and still is) a great trad-climbing destination. These days, Smith Rock draws climbers from both walks of life, and it is generally considered the sport-climbing mecca of the Northwest.

There are about 1500 routes, most sport, on the volcanic welded tuff cliffs huddled around the Crooked River. Smith is home to the country's first 5.14a and first 5.14c, but the area is better known for its classic climbs of all grades, beginner to intermediate to elite.

There are many routes sporting high first bolts on friable rock, so be sure to bring a stick clip. The early routes tend to feel more runout than today's sport climbers are used to. Take some time to adjust to the area and learn to read the rock on the easier climbs.

Techniques to learn here: Climbs are vertical and technical, and thus Smith is a premier area to hone classic face-climbing technique: learning how to *really* stand on your feet, climb in balance, and find the perfect body position to do the next move.

Routes are finger-intensive: crimpers and tiny pockets. Warm up well.

Where: Smith Rocks is located about 30 minutes from Bend along the Crooked River. You can't miss it.

When: Climbing year-round is possible but not necessarily pleasant. The summers can be extremely hot and the winters cold. It is possible to chase the sun/shade to stay comfortable. The weather can change quickly within a single day, so be prepared.

Other Northwest sport crags: Riggins and the City of Rocks, Idaho; Little Si, Exit 38, Frenchman Coulee, and the crags around Leavenworth, all in Washington.

INTERNATIONAL FLAVOR

The best places to go sport climbing may be abroad. The limestone of France (and most of Europe) is special, and every sport climber must make at least one pilgrimage to experience it. Obviously, with hundreds of foreign destinations out there this list is not comprehensive, but these three areas are amazing places to start. Bon voyage!

CÉÜSE, FRANCE

Céüse, a 2-mile-long cliff band crowning the top of an idyllic hillside in the French countryside, is widely considered one of the best sport-climbing destinations in the world. The recognition is largely due to the perfect rock here: blue, gray, and gold lime-

Traveling to a new area and getting to sample new rock is one of the greatest gifts offered by the climbing lifestyle.

stone that is solid, clean, and riddled with pockets. There are over 200 routes, from 5.8 to 5.15a, with most in the 5.10 to 5.12a range. You will need twenty quickdraws to do many of the classically long routes, not to mention a 70-meter rope. Céüse has garnered a reputation for having long runouts between bolts, giving many climbs an adventurous feel, but the steep rock makes the falls safe. To reach the climbing, you must hike one hour straight uphill.

Techniques to learn here: Céüse will hone your face-climbing technique on pockets, dishes, and edges like nowhere else. Céüse is also a great place to onsight if you have the fitness needed to climb gently overhanging rock for 35 meters. And if you don't, you'll get that fitness by climbing here!

Where: Céüse is just outside of the tiny town of Gap, in Southeastern France in the Haute-Alpes region. Most climbers camp at the Les Guérins campground.

When: At an altitude of 6500 feet, Céüse is best in the summer months, but the season extends from April to November. The wall is shaded in the afternoon. Afternoon thunderstorms mandate always bringing a raincoat with you.

Other sport crags in France: Les Gorges du Verdon, Buoux, Les Calanques, Orpierre.

EL POTRERO CHICO, MEXICO

Head just south of the border and you'll find one of the best multipitch sport-climbing destinations in North America. The 2000-foot big walls of El Potrero are home to classic moderate routes like the 11-pitch *Space Boyz* (5.10d), and technical, demanding lines like the 12-pitch *El Sendero Luminoso* (5.12d). There are well over 500 routes in the area, most in the 5.8 to 5.11 range. The rock on many of the routes is bullet limestone, but on some of the longer, more adventurous climbs, the rock quality deteriorates and can be loose.

El Potrero annually draws an eclectic and vibrant contingent of international climbers, especially right around New Year's Eve. Surely one of the best reasons to visit this area is to enjoy the friendly climber scene and warm Mexican culture.

Techniques to learn here: The climbing tends to be just less than vertical, which makes El Potrero a great place to perfect your footwork. The multipitch routes of El Potrero demand knowledge of techniques not covered in this book, including but not limited to routefinding, rappeling, climbing loose rock, belaying a second from above, and building anchors. That said, with proper knowledge of these skills, you will find El Potrero to be a fantastic introduction to multipitch climbing. And if you're not up to tackling the big routes, there are hundreds of excellent single-pitch excursions, too.

Where: The canyon is located just 30 minutes north of the city of Monterrey, Mexico—a 4-hour drive south from the border at Laredo, Texas.

When: Midwinter, from December to February.

KALYMNOS, GREECE

The Greek island of Kalymnos (*cal-im-nos*) is a relatively new climbing destination that boasts well over 500 climbs at over forty different crags. The limestone is varied and unique, offering easy slabs, steep walls, and massive caves with many stalactites (tufas). Bring fifteen draws and a 70-meter rope.

Fly into Kalymnos on a charter flight from Athens. Once you reach the island, expect to stay in luxurious accommodations that abut the turquoise waters of the Aegean Sea and are walking distance from the climbing—for less than 20 euros a day.

Techniques to learn here: Kalymnos has it all, but the region's most distinct ingredient is learning to climb upside down through a maze of stalactites. Many of these tufa formations are juggy, but they can also be hollow and make a "dong!" sound if you kick them too hard. Sometimes you'll find your legs wrapped around a tufa the size of a totem pole, which affords you a no-hands rest!

Where: twenty miles west of Turkey, Kalymnos is a part of the Dodecanese Islands in the Aegean Sea.

When: It's possible to climb here year-round, though the best months are in the fall and spring.

Glossary

anchor: The two bolts, usually equipped with chains or fixed lowering gear, at the top of a route. The anchor is where the climb ends, and the goal in sport climbing is to reach the anchor without falling.

arête: This rock feature is an edge pointing out from the wall and defined by the joining of two planes of rock. An arête can be blunt, round, or sharp.

backstep: Using the outside edge of your foot to stand on a hold.

belay: The technique used by a belayer to hold a rope in order to arrest a falling climber.

belay device: The device a belayer uses to hold the rope. There are two basic types of belay devices: passive/standard and autolocking. An autolocking belay device is best for sport climbing.

beta: Any information about how to do a specific climb.

bolt: Permanent protection drilled into the rock. Bolts are outfitted with hangers that make it possible to clip a quickdraw to them. Modern sport climbs use bolts for protection.

brake hand: The dominant hand, used to prevent the rope from sliding unchecked through a belay device. Never take your brake hand off the rope.

bucket: See *jug*.

carabiner (also biner): The aluminum snap link used for clipping. Carabiners come in a variety of designs such as wire-gate, closed-gate, bent-gate, D-shaped, oval-shaped, pear-shaped, and locking.

cleaning a route: The technique used to take one's quickdraws off a climb. After reaching the anchor, the belayer lowers the climber down while he retrieves his quickdraws.

cleaning an anchor: The technique of untying at an anchor to thread the rope through the fixed metal links. Also, *threading the chains*.

chalk: Magnesium-carbonate dust applied to hands to keep them dry and improve grip.

choss: Rock of inferior quality. Be careful of climbing in chossy areas: rocks could break, injuring you or your belayer.

corner: See *dihedral*.

crag: A wall with a collection of routes.

crimper: Small edge just wide enough for fingertips to hang onto it. One "crimps" on a crimper. You can grab a crimper in one of three positions: full-crimp, half-crimp, and open-hand.

crux: The most difficult section of a climb.

dihedral: A vertical corner feature formed by the intersection of two planes of rock. A dihedral is the opposite of an arête. Also, *corner* or *open book*.

draw: See *quickdraw*.

drop knee: The technique of placing your foot onto a foothold and rotating your knee so that it points downward.

dynamic rope: A rope that stretches in a fall. Dynamic ropes, as opposed to static ropes, are used for free climbing.

dyno: A "dynamic" move where a climber jumps and "sticks" a distant hold.

figure eight (retraced): A knot used to attach a climber to the end of the rope. A figure eight is tied to a harness.

figure eight on a bight: A figure eight tied in the middle of the rope. It has various applications in sport climbing, and is usually used when cleaning a route.

flash: Sending a route on your first try with beta.

flash pump: The feeling of swollen, aching forearms that occurs on the first route of the day. Avoiding the flash pump involves warming up slower, on easier routes.

free climbing: Using your hands and feet to climb up a rock face.

free soloing: Free climbing a route without the safety of a rope.

Gaston: Best described as a side pull that faces the wrong way. This is an edge/crimper that is held with the hand in a thumb-down position, making the elbow point up/out to the side.

gripped: Being terrified to the point that you don't want to let go.

hangdogging: A style of climbing where one hangs on bolts in order to figure out the moves.

harness: A climber wears a harness made of webbing around his body to attach himself to the rope.

heel hook: Foot technique where a heel is placed on an edge/foothold and used by pulling down with the hamstring.

hueco: A large hole in the rock.

jug: A large hold. Also, *bucket*.

kneebar: Locking the lower half of your leg in a gap by pressing with the knee and pushing with the foot against two opposing rock features.

leading: Climbing up a route and clipping the rope to the bolts using quickdraws for protection. Also, *the sharp end.*

lieback: Technique of pushing on a face with the feet while pulling with the hands on an opposing edge or crack.

mantel: Moving onto a shelf of rock by pressing down on it with one or both palms until you are able to stand on the "mantel." Like getting out of a pool.

mono: A one-finger pocket.

move: A single "move" is placing a hand or foot onto the next rock hold.

onsight: The style of climbing a route on your first try without any beta.

open book: See *dihedral.*

pitch: A pitch is a section of rock that has a definitive start and a definitive end at an anchor. In sport climbing you will mostly be doing "single-pitch" routes, which are usually about half of a rope's length. Multipitch routes go up cliffs that are longer than one rope length and are outside the scope of this book.

pinch: A handhold that one squeezes between the fingers and thumb.

pocket: A small hole in the wall that one grabs with the fingers. Pockets come in two-finger and three-finger sizes. A one-finger pocket is called a *mono.*

project: The route that you are currently trying to redpoint.

projecting: See *working a route.*

protection: In trad climbing the protection is removable gear such as cams and nuts that are placed in the rock to catch a climber's fall. In sport climbing the protection is the preplaced bolts. Also, *pro.*

pumped: A buildup of lactic acid in the forearms caused by the fatigue of free climbing.

quickdraw: Two carabiners connected with a nylon or Spectra sling, or "runner." A quickdraw has a definitive top and bottom carabiner. The top carabiner clips to the bolt hanger, while you clip the rope to the bottom carabiner. Also, *draw.*

rappel: Descent technique where a climber uses a belay device to slide down a rope.

redpoint: Climbing a route without falling or resting on gear after previously rehearsing the moves.

redpoint crux: The section of difficult moves near the top of a route that gives one difficulty on the redpoint attempt.

roof: An overhanging feature that juts out 90 degrees from the vertical rock face. A roof could be small or tremendous in size.

route: A route is a rock climb. All routes have a name and a grade.

runout: When the distance between two bolts is far, a climb is said to be "runout."

send: Successfully climbing a route without falling or resting on gear.

shaking out: The resting technique of holding your arm out away from the rock and shaking it in order to reduce the feeling of being pumped.

side pull: A hold that faces away from the body that you can use by pulling toward yourself.

slab: A route that is less steep, typically under 90 degrees.

sloper: A hold that must be gripped with

an open hand because of its sloping nature. Using a sloper depends on friction, balance, and body tension.

smear: A sloping foothold: the ball of the foot is "pasted" onto the surface in order to gain purchase.

soft catch: A belaying technique that prevents a falling climber from swinging into the wall.

stem: A body position of standing on oblique holds, such as in a dihedral, by pushing in opposite directions with the feet.

stick clip: A telescopic pole with an apparatus at one end that allows you to clip quickdraws to bolts and ropes to quickdraws.

technical: A description of a route that requires technique. Technical routes tend to have small footholds that require a slow, precise style of climbing. Vertical routes tend to be described as technical. Overhanging routes, while requiring good technique, are not usually described as technical. Also, *techy.*

the sharp end: See *leading.*

threading the chains: See *cleaning an anchor.*

toe hook: Wrapping the top of the foot up or around a rock feature.

top rope: When a climber has the security of a rope from above.

undercling: A down-facing hold that is grabbed palms up.

whipper: A big fall.

working a route: The process of figuring out moves by hangdogging, with the goal of one day redpointing the climb. Also, *projecting.*

Z-clip: An incorrect way to clip. The leader pulls up slack from below a lower quickdraw and clips it to the higher one.

RATING COMPARISON CHART FOR SPORT CLIMBING

French	YDS	French	YDS
1	5.1	7a	5.11d
2	5.2	7a+	5.12a
2+	5.3	7b	5.12b
3-	5.4	7b+	5.12c
3	5.5	7c	5.12d
3+	5.6	7c+	5.13a
4	5.7	8a	5.13b
4+	5.8	8a+	5.13c
5	5.9	8b	5.13d
5+	5.10a	8b+	5.14a
6a	5.10b	8c	5.14b
6a+	5.10c	8c+	5.14c
6b	5.10d	9a	5.14d
6b+	5.11a	9a+	5.15a
6c	5.11b	9b	5.15b
6c+	5.11c	9b+	5.15c

INDEX

About the Author

Since 2005, Andrew Bisharat has been the senior editor of *Rock and Ice* magazine, where you can find his column "Tuesday Night Bouldering." He is an accomplished all-around climber who has achieved difficult sport, trad, bouldering, big-wall, mixed, ice and alpine ascents. Bisharat graduated from Tufts University in 2003 with a degree in political science, and he now lives in Carbondale, Colorado. This is his first book.

© Marni Mattner/www.mattnerphotography.com

THE MOUNTAINEERS, founded in 1906, is a nonprofit outdoor activity and conservation club, whose mission is "to explore, study, preserve, and enjoy the natural beauty of the outdoors...." Based in Seattle, Washington, the club is now one of the largest such organizations in the United States, with seven branches throughout Washington State.

The Mountaineers sponsors both classes and year-round outdoor activities in the Pacific Northwest, which include hiking, mountain climbing, ski-touring, snowshoeing, bicycling, camping, canoeing and kayaking, nature study, sailing, and adventure travel. The club's conservation division supports environmental causes through educational activities, sponsoring legislation, and presenting informational programs.

All club activities are led by skilled, experienced volunteers, who are dedicated to promoting safe and responsible enjoyment and preservation of the outdoors.

If you would like to participate in these organized outdoor activities or the club's programs, consider a membership in The Mountaineers. For information and an application, write or call The Mountaineers, Club Headquarters, 7700 Sand Point Way NE, Seattle, WA 98115; 206-521-6001. You can also visit the club's website at www.mountaineers.org or contact The Mountaineers via email at clubmail@mountaineers.org.

The Mountaineers Books, an active, nonprofit publishing program of the club, produces guidebooks, instructional texts, historical works, natural history guides, and works on environmental conservation. All books produced by The Mountaineers Books fulfill the club's mission. Visit www.mountaineersbooks.org to find details about all our titles and the latest author events, as well as videos, web clips, links, and more!

The Mountaineers Books
1001 SW Klickitat Way, Suite 201
Seattle, WA 98134
800-553-4453
mbooks@mountaineersbooks.org

The Mountaineers Books is proud to be a corporate sponsor of The Leave No Trace Center for Outdoor Ethics, whose mission is to promote and inspire responsible outdoor recreation through education, research, and partnerships. The Leave No Trace program is focused specifically on human-powered (nonmotorized) recreation.

Leave No Trace strives to educate visitors about the nature of their recreational impacts, as well as offer techniques to prevent and minimize such impacts. Leave No Trace is best understood as an educational and ethical program, not as a set of rules and regulations.

For more information, visit www.lnt.org, or call 800-332-4100.

OTHER TITLES YOU MIGHT ENJOY FROM THE MOUNTAINEERS BOOKS

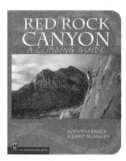

Red Rock Canyon: A Climbing Guide
Brock, McMillen
More than 1500 sport and trad routes
in the popular Red Rocks area

Rock Climbing: Mastering Basic Skills
Luebben
Trad climbing instruction for
beginner to intermediate climbers

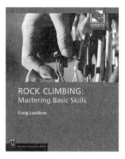

Climbing: Training for Peak Performance
Soles
Training programs and goals for all
levels of climbing expertise

Alpine Climbing: Techniques to Take You Higher
Cosley and Houston
Techniques for speed and efficiency
over rock, snow, ice, and glaciers

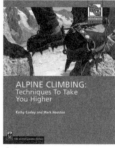

Mountaineering: The Freedom of the Hills 7th Edition
The Mountaineers
The climber's bible—complete, authoritative
instruction on mountaineering

THE MOUNTAINEERS BOOKS